In Search of the Wild Dulcimer

In Search of the Wild Dulcimer

ROBERT FORCE & ALBERT d'OSSCHÉ

Artist—Carole Palmer

VINTAGE BOOKS

A Division of Random House/New York

VINTAGE BOOKS EDITION 1974
First Edition

Copyright © 1974 by Albert d'Ossché and
Robert Force, Jr.
Artwork Copyright © 1974 by Random House, Inc.
All rights reserved under International and Pan-American
Copyright Conventions. Published in the United States by
Random House, Inc., New York, and simultaneously
distributed in Canada by Random House
of Canada Limited, Toronto.

Library of Congress Cataloging in Publication Data

Force, Robert.
    In search of the wild dulcimer.

    "Books and records of interest": p.
    1. Dulcimer—Methods—Self instruction.
    I. D'Ossché, Albert, joint author. II. Title.
MT634.D9F7   787'.9   74-8909
ISBN 0-394-71064-9

Manufactured in the United States of America

Dedicated to
RICHARD FARIÑA AND PAUL CLAYTON,
who taught us through their music

Special thanks to our friend J. R. Beall

Introduction

I don't rightly know if I'm supposed to be introducing the authors, this book, or dulcimers. So I'll just go back to when I met Al and Bob, and start there.

I was sitting on a bench after performing at the '73 Smithsonian Folklife Festival when down the road came two fellows picking dulcimers in a way I had never heard. I called out and asked them to come over and play something. They obliged, introduced themselves, and shortly we were talking about music, dulcimers, and life in general.

A few weeks later I received a letter from them saying that this book had been accepted for publication, and would I write an introduction...something of what we talked about when we first met.

Well, if my memory serves me right, we talked about a lot of things. But, most important, I said that music is just the way you play it. Don't be afraid to go your own way musically. Keep adapting songs, experimenting, and doing things differently. That's what its all about...expressing yourself in a pleasing way, and getting what's inside, out.

For many of you this book will be not only an introduction to dulcimers but to music as well. Keep in mind that this book is something you can work with, something that will enable you to help yourself make your own music—and all you have to do is take the time to do it.

Charlie Monroe

Contents

Introduction   vii

Foreword   xi

1   YOU'LL FIND THAT WITH DULCIMERS…   1

2   TERMS AND TUNING   11

3   HOLDING AND RHYTHM AND
    HOLDING A RHYTHM   27

4   MELODY AND THE MIXOLYDIAN MODE   39

5   ODDS AND ENDS OF TECHNIQUE   51

6   FIVE MORE MODES   59

7   PICKIN'   65

8   CHORDING   75

9   MORE ODDS AND ENDS:
    The Locrian and Other Modes
    Singing, Songsmithing, and Minstrelsy
    An Apology and a Poem   87

10   PLAYING WITH A GUITAR   95

11   SOME USEFUL CHARTS, BOOKS,
     AND RECORDS OF INTEREST   99

Foreword

So you're interested in dulcimers.

But like us, you may not have had much success in finding information to help you learn to play the instrument.

Although there are a number of books about the playing and the building of dulcimers, none of them really clears the way for persons with no musical background who come in search of something that will help them make music.

This book is somewhat different from the other dulcimer books you may have seen, for we approach the dulcimer—and dulcimer music—in a new way. Over the past few years we have found that the dulcimer can be played in a contemporary guitar style, allowing the musician to stand up if he so desires. Traditionally you play the dulcimer sitting down, but we found this style placed limitations on what could be done rhythmically and melodically.

Our desire to play the dulcimer as a contemporary musical instrument caused us to devise particular techniques, and this book is nothing more than an analysis of these techniques, along with some encouragement for those of you who are just beginning to explore the world of making your own music.

For the past few years we have traveled around the United States and parts of Europe playing dulcimer music, building dulcimers, and helping others with their playing. Often the stimulus for writing has come from the many people with whom we have spent time, played music, and shared what we know. Early in the process of writing we realized that people teach themselves best by doing. So, to this end, we offer you these elements of dulcimer playing that are easily learned and put into practice by almost anyone.

We explain different techniques and styles that you can use in your playing, be it ever so simple in the beginning. And we offer information that we believe is vital to a real understanding of the dulcimer—a close examination of the various modal tunings, historical comments, and finger positions for playing chords.

When we started our search for how to play the dulcimer, we knew few songs and very little, if anything, about music. So all our explanations are in layman's terms, and any strange music terminologies are defined in context so you won't get hung-up. If a passage on technique (or anything else) is confusing at first, read it aloud, slowly. Think...use your imagination.

The songs we recommend for practicing techniques are ones all of us know. We believe that once you are familiar with the instrument, and what it can and cannot do, and once you are beginning to play it, you'll find that learning songs from musicians, records, or other dulcimer books will come easily.

As music is a process of sharing, so too is this book. If you discover new tunings, develop special techniques, find weird strings, picks, or anything at all in which you think other prople would be interested, let us know what you've found or developed, and we'll pass the information on.

There is a certain magic about the dulcimer. It's hard to define, but if it's touched you, you know what it is. Keep this magic alive, and your music will take on form and substance, will grow and develop from within.

Shanti.

Bob Force and Al d'Ossché

1
You'll
Find That
with Dulcimers...

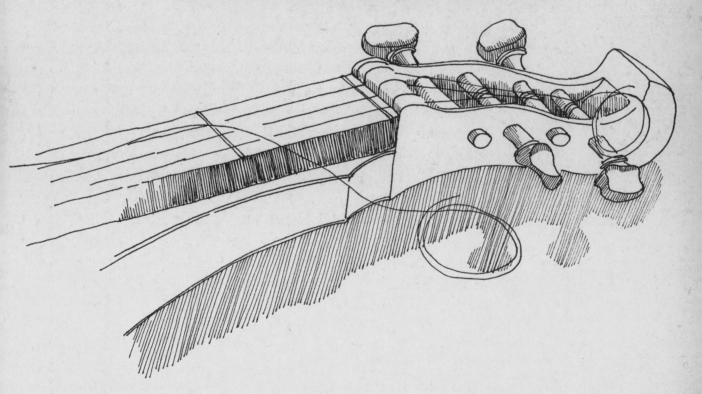

...the sizes and shapes and the number of strings are as varied as the cultures in which the instrument finds its origins. There remains a great deal of room for research and speculation about these origins, and also about how the dulcimer ended up in the Appalachian Mountain regions of the United States.

"Appalachian" is the name given to a series of composite mountain ranges stretching from New Hampshire, Maine and Vermont, through Virginia and West Virginia, and on into North Carolina, Tennessee, and Northern Georgia. (Some people even consider the Ozarks of Arkansas as part of the Appalachians.) In any case, the Appalachians, the oldest mountains on the North American continent, are far less rugged and altogether more hospitable than those which dominate the Western regions of the United States. And since the Appalachians mark the western boundary of the Eastern seaboard, they formed the first major physical barrier to westward expansion in colonial times and provided a major area for settlement.

Into these mountains came the adventurers, the criminals, the rugged individualists, and the general run-of-the-mill romantics from Western Europe. We'll leave the rest of the story to a course in United States History, but sometime, after the trees were felled and the land divided, people remembered their European traditions. They built instruments like those from back home, stringed instruments that sounded like Scotch-Irish bagpipes, appropriate for local "get-it-ons" and gatherings. There was no single inventor of the dulcimer—just a gentle synthesis from many cultures that led to instruments found today in many shapes and sizes, but all known by one name, "dulcimer."

And to distinguish this new instrument from the English Hammered Dulcimer, a zither-type instrument played with mallets, it became known as the "plucked Southern Appalachian Mountain Dulcimer."

To meet the social and musical demands of a

rough-and-tumble, lively, hand-clapping, foot-stomping, knee-slapping "Sattidy Nite," the dulcimer had to be rugged. From the extensive collection of Ann Grimes of Granville, Ohio, there is one dulcimer that immediately comes to mind because it has a 2 by 4 for a fretboard and bent-over spikes for frets. But this was more the exception than the rule, for the common dulcimer was a lap-sized instrument. Unable to compete adequately in volume and versatility with guitars, banjos, and fiddles, it slowly faded back into the hills and was considered all but a dead end by the 1930's.

Since then, people like John Jacob Niles and Jean Ritchie have done much to repopularize the dulcimer, but primarily as a soft-spoken, lyrical solo instrument. Following the folk revival of the sixties and the post-'67 search for ethnic roots and Americana, however, the dulcimer has received greater attention as an instrument to be reckoned with. Central to this increasing interest have been Richard Fariña, Paul Clayton, and Howie Mitchell, to name just a few. Each in his own way, with songs new and old, has infused new vitality into the near-forgotten dulcimer.

Our basic concern is teaching people to play the dulcimer in a contemporary manner. But even though we don't come from Appalachia, there is much we have learned from its musical traditions and techniques. And to those of you who are in the process of discovering the dulcimer for yourselves, take a good long look at the word "folk" because, really, it means you and what you do.

Your instrument...what does it look like? (If you don't own one yet, consider this section "What to look for when you buy one.")

Generally, you'll find the Appalachian Mountain Dulcimer in five basic shapes, with a variety of stringing patterns, and practically any number of strings. Most commonly, dulcimers appear in three-, four-, five-, or six-string arrangements. Only one type is truly "multi-stringed."

HOURGLASS DULCIMER

NOTE THE FIVE TUNERS ON
THIS VIOLIN SHAPED DULCIMER

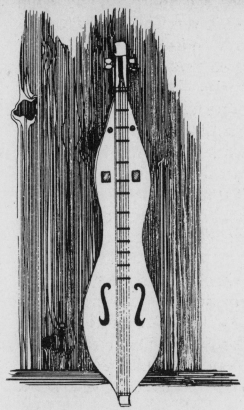

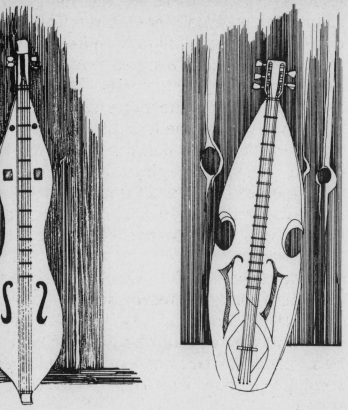

TEARDROP AND
ELLIPTICAL DULCIMERS

LUTE SHAPED DULCIMER

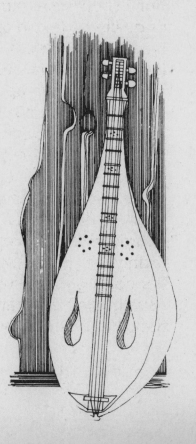

The greater the instrument's depth, the greater its bass response; therefore, the hourglass and violin shapes, which usually are not very deep, tend to produce less bass and slightly more treble. Moreover, they create a kind of a stereo effect by separating the bass and treble modulations. They are somewhat like the sitar in this effect; the narrow channel at mid-instrument blocks the larger functioning frequencies of sound (bass) and permits the tighter frequencies (treble) to pass through to the smaller chamber toward the head of the instrument.

The teardrop shaped dulcimer, with a sound chamber one and a half to two inches deep, provides a good balance.

This and the hourglass dulcimer are the most common, particularly in three- or four-string arrangements.

The elliptical shape is also about two inches deep. Due to its symmetry, its sound quality, when visualized, resembles two concentric circular ripples converging in a pond. This shape produces a very round sound.

The lute shaped dulcimer, found with great variation in depth and number of strings, is the rarest type of dulcimer. Some are as shallow as the elliptical or teardrop dulcimers, and others are as deep as ten inches. Some lute shaped dulcimers have four strings, and others have up to ten or more. All have a very rich, full sound, but they are not suited for fast tempos and tend to sound like a piano played with the sustaining pedal depressed.

Two "specialty" instruments are the courting dulcimer and something we call the "wall dulcimer." The courting dulcimer is usually rectangular with two fretboards placed in opposite directions. Two lovers sit facing each other, rub knees, and play dulcimer duets. It's not a good instrument to learn on because you usually can't maintain the needed concentration. And then there is the "wall dulcimer." Some people call

this instrument the "Flatland-Tourist Special" or the "Folk Antique." Aside from the few genuine antique instruments, most of these dulcimers are prevalent in areas where "traditional" means "looks made with the teeth." People who buy these dulcimers usually hang them on rec-room walls in suburban bungalows. If you have one of these, take it off the wall, dust it off, fix it up, give it new strings, and play it.

Each one of these shapes has a particular character and sound, and surely one of them will fit your hands, ears, and head.

So you've gone out and found a friend's friend's dulcimer. Or maybe you ordered one through the mail. Or built one for yourself...or had an instrument maker build you one. Then again, maybe you were lucky enough to find one in some outlandishly out-of-the-way "shoppe." But how do you know if it's any good?

Okay. Let's start with the wood.

We fuss a lot over the wood from which an instrument is constructed. It's very important, and we tap on the wood to hear its tone. We hum into the sound holes, and generally make sure the dulcimer will take all the use we have in store for it. Really though, we're fanatics when it comes to dulcimers, and many of our tests probably produce no tangible results.

Once again, it comes back to individual taste. A good hardwood usually is best because it gives a "brighter" tone than softwoods. Also, some woods have more eye-appealing figuring and coloration than others. A spruce top sometimes improves the quality of the sound.

But there is one definite thing to say about wood: the more you play it, the better it sounds. For this reason older instruments are often more valuable and sought-after than newer ones. When an instrument is played, the constant vibration within the sound chamber alters the physical structure of the woods cells—some shrink and change shape, some elongate—and the sound of the instrument slowly becomes richer.

You want to get as well-constructed an instrument as you can. Pick the dulcimer up and check to see if there are any cracks in the wood or along the seams where the parts have been glued together. If there are cracks, push gently on one side and see if the wood depresses. If it does, it will mean a repair. If the crack does not depress, chances are that it cracked during construction and was repaired at that time.

Tap on it. Shake it. Does anything rattle? Maybe a brace or gluing block is loose. Check the overall gluing job.

Take a look down the fretboard's length, end to end. Does it have any curves or dips in it? Is it lopsided? If it is not straight and flat, your strings will be at odd distances from the frets, and this can create problems in playing and sound quality.

Depress the strings individually and strum...no matter what the sound. Do any of the frets "buzz"? Check each string at each fret along the entire length of the fretboard. If there are buzzes, they can be eliminated either by raising the bridge, which means making a new one, or by carefully filing the offending frets down a trifle with a very fine surfaced flat mill file. If nothing works to solve your problems with the dulcimer in question, get rid of it, don't buy it, or be prepared for a major overhaul before you've even started.

Do the tuning pegs turn easily? If they are wooden "friction pegs" as on a violin or viola, look to see if they are tapered to fit the peg holes. If they are mechanical (untapered) pegs as on a guitar, twist them to see if there is enough play in the gearing for them to move smoothly—you'll be doing a great deal of this, so you might as well start now.

Does the instrument have an adjustable bridge? Not always, but most often, you'll have problems with chording if it doesn't. For instance, your bass

string has a thicker diameter than the other strings, and the bass side of the bridge needs to be set at a slight angle toward the tail of the instrument. If the bridge is adjustable, you can fix this easily by moving it with your fingers.

Are there a few inches of instrument behind the bridge? Or does the instrument end at the bridge itself? Having a few extra inches behind the bridge on which to rest your hand or forearm can be a help.

Are all the strings over the fretboard? This may sound strange, but some traditional instruments have a very narrow fretboard, with the drone strings (the middle and the bass) parallel to the fretboard but not over any of the frets. If you're going to have strings on the instrument, you might as well be able to make notes with them, so we'd recommend a full-sized fretboard, wide enough to accommodate all the strings.

Your instrument's sound holes may be any shape. They should be large enough to let out the sound without unduly decreasing the vibration area of the top; that is, your instrument produces its sounds from the resonant vibrations of the top. The back and

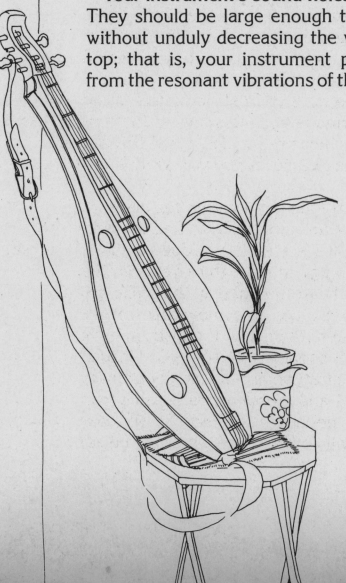

sides contain "color," and amplify the sound while pushing it out through the sound holes. If your sound holes are too small, you lose volume. If they are too large, you end up with a brash tone.

Are all the notes on the fretboard true? It's quite important that all the notes, even the ones way up the fretboard toward the bridge, be true and not sharp or flat due to incorrect fret placement.

Equidistant between the "nut" and the bridge (see the illustration on nomenclature on p.10) is one fret (usually the seventh) which when lightly touched will produce a harmonic tone. To make the harmonic, a clear, bell-like sound, touch the string with a finger of the left hand without depressing it to the fret. Quickly pluck the string with your right hand while simultaneously lifting your left finger off the string from over the fret.

Okay. Try this on the first string, or first two (unison) strings if you are dealing with a four-string dulcimer. It may take you a few times to get the bell-like note, but when you depress the string to the fret over which you found the bell-tone, the note you get off the fret should be exactly the same sound as the bell-tone harmonic. If the note you get upon depressing and plucking the string is not the same as the harmonic tone, carefully move the bridge a little forward or backward until the two notes match closely, if not exactly.

Experiment. Next try the harmonic on the eleventh fret from the nut. Do the same thing to find the bell-tone. And when you've gotten the bridge adjusted, depress the first string(s) onto the third fret from the nut and, moving up the fretboard, play the scale, do-re-me-fa-sol-la-ti-do. Do the notes now follow true?

Also, a strap-peg at both ends of the instrument is good for attaching a shoulder strap. If your instrument does not have strap-pegs, you can put them in yourself. Both metal and wooden pegs usually can be purchased at a good music store. If you get wooden pegs, you will have to bore a hole (or holes)

in the instrument and glue them in. Metal strap pegs screw into the instrument. So do what you think is best.

When you are looking at dulcimers, you might want to drag along a friend who knows something about guitars. No doubt he can help you with any of these considerations. You should be able to find a good-quality, hand-crafted instrument for right around eighty-five dollars. Or you can make one from a kit for about thirty dollars. If you are open to a suggestion: try to find a four-string dulcimer with a fretboard and string arrangement like the one illustrated.

If you notice any differences between your dulcimer's fretboard and the one in the illustration, you have either a variation of the standard dulcimer with an eight-note scale or a longer fretboard than the one shown. We consider many of the variations we have seen to be confusing and more trouble than they are worth because "extra" frets cloud the concept of the instrument and the "diatonic systems" known as <u>modes.</u>

The four-string variety with its double "lead" string simply provides a little more sound than the three-string dulcimer, and we think you'll find it to be a bit more pleasing.

So you've found a dulcimer, checked it over, and like its sound. And because you already know that the more it is played the better it will sound, we'd best get on with learning to do so.

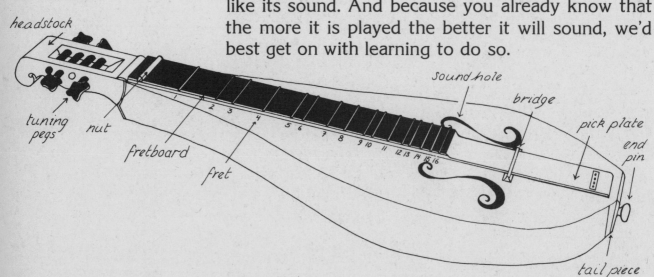

Nomenclature

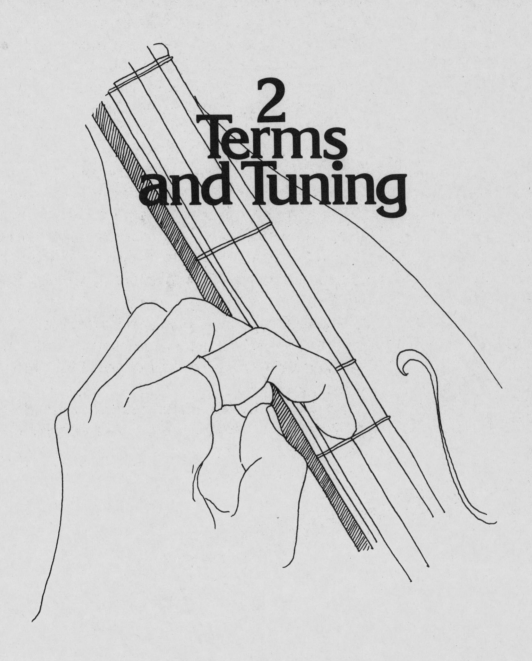

2
Terms
and Tuning

To avoid entering a stage of mumbo jumbo, let's make sure we're all talking about the same thing at the same time. Don't be baffled by unfamiliar terms, because we will use them in context, and as we go along you'll find they will all fall readily into place.

Our teaching technique is based on the four-string diatonic scale (eight-note) dulcimer like the one in the nomenclature illustration. We'll start with tuning. And in order to tune, we'd better find out which string is which and how to restring in case one breaks.

Place your dulcimer on your lap, with the head of the instrument to your left. (If you are left-handed, we apologize, but you'll have to reverse everything from here on in. However, you may be used to doing this.)

Your dulcimer may not look anything like the one in the nomenclature illustration, but in general, it will have the same parts. Your dulcimer may have more frets, a differently shaped headstock (peg-head), smaller sound holes, a different kind of bridge, and no strap peg. But it does have strings, and we'll number the strings, number 1 being closest to you, lightest to thickest.

We call the first two strings either the "unison" or "melody" strings and number them 1 and 2. The middle string is number 3, and the bass or octave string, numbered 4, is on the bottom. If you have a dulcimer strung in another manner, it would be best to standardize to this string arrangement for the purposes of this book.

COMMON FOUR-STRING ARRANGEMENT

Some four-string dulcimers are strung equidistantly. You can make a set of unisons by bringing the second string closer to the first. Using a pocket knife or fine-toothed saw, simply cut an additional groove on the nut and bridge, imitating the slant and depth of the other cuts. Then reposition the string.

EQUIDISTANT STRING ARRANGEMENT

Another string arrangement you might try sometime places the unisons between the middle string (3), which moves over to the first position, and the bass. We've seen this arrangement on a number of three- and four-string dulcimers coming from the Ozarks and Vermont.

Remember that a three-string dulcimer is like a four-string, except that it has only one melody string. If your melody string is not on the outside closest to you, move it and then you'll have a first, a third, and a fourth string.

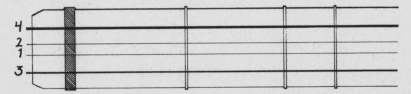

OZARK STRINGING

If you have a five-string dulcimer, you have various options, depending on how your five strings are arranged. If you have two unisons, fine. The other three strings may then be arranged any way you wish or left as is. The extra string (designated by an asterisk in the illustration) is another melody string that drones along with the middle and bass string. You can keep it on the instrument, move it near the bass string, or take it off. This five-string arrangement is prevalent in the eastern Tennessee/Great Smoky Mountains area of Appalachia, as is the violin-shaped dulcimer.

FIVE-STRING ARRANGEMENT

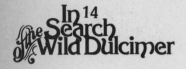

The six-string dulcimer, also known as the church dulcimer because of its fuller tone, and its use in small country churches, is found throughout Appalachia. The middle and bass strings are doubled. If you happen to have a six-string dulcimer, you can leave the additional strings on. In the beginning you will have more strings to tune correctly, and the increased "pick drag" caused by these additional strings makes it somewhat more difficult to explore fast tempos, but do what you will.

SIX-STRING ARRANGEMENT

Not very often, but sometimes, you will come across a six-string dulcimer strung like a twelve-string guitar. Instead of two identical middle and bass strings, it will have a lighter-gauge string strung to a pitch an octave higher than the string it is duplicating. This is more or less a customized sound—something you may want to get into later on.

If you have a lute dulcimer, the first three to six strings may be in any of the combinations mentioned previously. You'll have to adjust accordingly. We suggest you remove the additional strings while learning to play because they tend to sustain the sound and hinder the development of a rhythmic playing style. Then again, for playing slower, more traditional music, the lute dulcimer is very rich and is the favorite of John Jacob Niles, a well-known dulcimer player and folk-song collector.

You can always return to stringing the dulcimer in whatever way you found it. If you want, and think it won't play too many games with your head, you can keep it in its original stringing arrangement and adapt our instructions as you go along. But really, the extra grooves and standard stringing will not only make the book easier to follow, but will increase the versatility of your instrument.

So now we know which string is which. But what about the strings themselves?

We'll begin tuning by using a standard type and gauge of string. Later you can customize your instrument to the pitch of your voice, with the help of the String Tone Tolerance Chart and Range and Tuning Guide in the back of this book. But for now we'll use five-string-banjo strings—two firsts, one second, and a fourth. If you buy them by the gauge, we recommend two .010's, a .012, and a .022. The fourth string (bass string) comes in wound and unwound varieties —you want the wound.

Furthermore, depending upon what kind of tailpiece and string attachment system you have, you can get either "ball-end" or "loop-end" strings. So check this out before you trot off and purchase strings with the wrong kind of end.

Remove your old strings. They may be new, but you never know, and most probably the ones that come with your instrument will be "dead, oh so dead," and will have a sound like spit hitting a cast-iron frying pan. You may as well learn how to change your strings now so when one breaks you'll know how to deal with the situation.

There is really only one truly efficient technique for putting strings on an instrument; however, there are at least three schools of thought on this matter. Some people are aghast at the thought of cutting off a string's excess length. They wind the string onto the tuning peg in a way that allows the excess length to dangle hither and yon, thereby preserving, as it were, the string's "soul"—while providing a convenient place to jam their filter cigarettes while playing. We call this the "Rock 'n' Roll String Syndrome." The second group also believes in a string's soul. They either wind the string completely onto the tuning peg (not very practical), or they wind the string around the peg several times and curl the excess length into a little circle (like it was when it came from the package) which clutters up the peg-head.

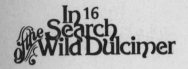

In our minds the simplest procedure is the most practical: wind the string once, twice, three times around the peg, and snip!

It makes no difference whether you have mechanical or friction peg tuners—the process is the same for both. When stringing an instrument, you might find needlenose pliers useful. Remember also that when you are finished stringing you will probably have to readjust your bridge if it is moveable.

Take the string out of the package and carefully uncurl it. Watch out for little knots or binds. Just loosen the curl and straighten it out to its full length. Start with the first unison string, then the bass, then the second unison, and finally the middle. If you remove one string at a time and replace it, you will minimize the chances of your bridge falling off or moving out of adjustment.

Okay. Insert the plain end of the string through the eye of the tuning peg and pull some of the string length through. Then attach the loop end to the tailpiece. If you have ball-end strings, pull the string through the eye of the peg until the ball end jams up against the tailpiece.

Keep the string loose, and gauge how much slack you will need to wind the string at least three times around the shaft of the tuning peg. Try to keep as much of a straight-line pull on the string as possible. Be careful not to crease it.

The best way to avoid this is to maintain an upward pull with your free hand, letting the string pass over the back of your hand and across the thumb and forefinger. As you wind the string down nearer to the fretboard, change your hand position so that without losing tension you are now holding it with the pads of your fingers.

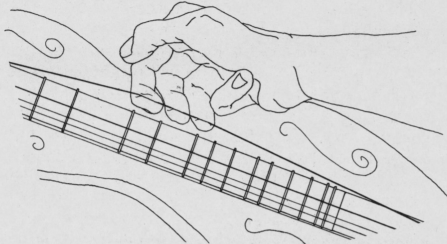

AS STRING WINDS CLOSER TO FRETBOARD, RIGHT HAND CHANGES POSITION UNTIL STRING IS ON TOP OF FINGERS

If you have friction pegs, make sure you wind the string over the top of the tuner, not from underneath. No matter what kind of tuners you have, it is important that you bind a little of the free end underneath the initial windings. Doing this will prevent the string from slipping through the peg-hole as you tighten it and bring it up to pitch.

STYLIZED CROSS-SECTION VIEW OF FRICTION PEG AND STRING WINDING —NOTE HOW THE WINDING BINDS ON TOP OF THE SMALL PIECE OF STRING TO KEEP THE STRING FROM COMING LOOSE

When using friction pegs, twist and turn them into the headstock. As you twist the peg into the hole, try to maintain an even pressure so that the peg "holds."

If a friction peg binds unnecessarily hard or "creaks" loudly, remove it and rub it on a dry bar of soap. Then, with regular soft school chalk, mark a ring around the parts that contact the wood of the headstock. This should make the peg turn very smoothly. If not, do it again. And remember, because friction pegs are individually tapered, they usually fit best into their original holes. So try not to get your pegs mixed up.

When you've wound the string to a moderate tightness and are sure it won't slip when you bring it up to pitch, snip off the excess length that dangles about, and you're finished.

So now you should be strung up...or out...or something. But don't worry whether you've done it right. For now, if it works, it's right.

Now take a close look at your fret scale. The one we'll be using is the eight-note diatonic scale which looks like this.

The short arrows indicate where additional frets would be if the dulcimer were a twelve-tone, or <u>chromatic</u>, instrument like the guitar or banjo. If your <u>dulcimer</u> has a variation of the diatonic scale, it will probably be a one-fret inclusion found at point A in the illustration—though any additional fret may be included at the whim of the instrument maker. Some builders place additional frets on the scale as half-frets extending under the unison strings and halfway across the fretboard. If your dulcimer has any or all of these "extra" or half-frets, you'll have to work a little harder by sometimes pretending that they're not there.

Okay. So we know which string is which, and how to attach them to a dulcimer.

Now we're going to learn a song called "Tuning" —ominous, isn't it? There is probably no greater task in store for you than to develop an "ear" for this. It takes a little time—unless you were born with a phenomenon called "perfect pitch"—so don't worry about it. Just buy a few extra sets of strings and you are ready for anything.

We are going to tune the dulcimer into the <u>Mix-</u>

olydian mode, which means we will have an open chord when all the strings are strummed without depressing any of them to the frets. The original starting tonality of the Mixolydian mode was the note G, but our five-string-banjo first strings (.010's) don't easily tune up to a treble, or mid-range, G. So we tune our unison strings to a tone somewhere around D, which is very pleasant and has some definite advantages for quick tuning into other modes. Therefore, our Mixolydian is going to be transposed to D.

In musical notation, our tuning looks like this:

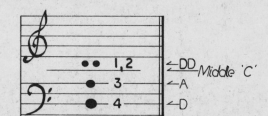

And on a piano, the notes we want to tune to are these:

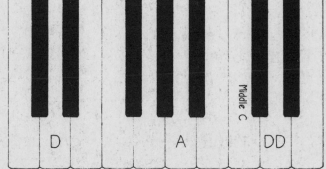

There remains nothing more for you to do except duplicate these notes on your strings. You can use the D of a reed pitch-pipe, but the sound "color" of a reed is different from that of a string, so it may throw you off a bit. A D tuning fork, a precise little device piano tuners use, can also help in finding the D tone.

Then again, if you know something about the piano or can work with a friend who will give you a D from his guitar, banjo, or fiddle, you're in business. But if there's no piano, guitar, or banjo around, or if a pitch pipe or tuning fork is unavailable, simply tune your unison strings to any note you think sounds good and is not too high for the strings. You might try a note from the mid-range of your singing voice, but whatever you do, your note should not be weak and watery—just a nice, fairly taut, clear note. Don't worry …the strings will let you know if you are tuning too high, so tune slowly.

The actual notes with which you are dealing are not half as important as the relationship between these notes. The "strongest" tonal relationship is the difference between <u>octaves</u> (D to DD)—when a note is eight tones above or below the note from which you start. For example, <u>do</u>-re-mi-fa-sol-la-ti-<u>do</u>.

The second strongest relationship is that of a fifth (D to A)—when a note is five tones away from the starting tone (<u>do</u>-re-mi-fa-<u>sol</u>-la-ti-do). The third strongest is when a note is four tones away from the starting tone, <u>sol</u> (A to DD), and is a <u>fourth</u>. In this case, our scale reads do-re-mi-fa-<u>sol</u>-la-ti-<u>do</u>.

When in tune, we have two tones an octave apart (the unisons and the bass) combined with two tones a fifth apart (the unisons and the middle string), as well as two tones a fourth apart (the middle string and the bass). And, nicely enough, it makes a chord—not a very sophisticated chord—but at least when struck open, it's easy to do.

You can tune and play your dulcimer all day long without ever having to know what <u>key</u> you're in or to what note your unisons are actually tuned. All "being in a key" does is allow you to relate where you are tuned and what you are doing to other musicians.

It is important to keep in mind that like a great many other things, notes and keys are really arbitrary values that have been standardized over the years for reference use. To put it another way: There's not much difference between a D above middle C that vibrates at 300 cycles per second and one that vibrates at the established standard of 294. When you consider that middle C itself is rated at 262 cycles per second, and that E, the note above D, is set at 330, a tone vibrating at 300 cycles isn't that far off.

To you, this tone of 300 cycles per second is just some tone, and a perfectly good one to tune to, at that. To someone with perfect pitch, it's a slightly sharp D...so why not?

We're going to describe our notation system for tuning. All you have to do is recognize tones an octave apart. This system has only a few rules, and by following them you will be able to tune successfully and play your dulcimer in every mode. Don't be afraid of breaking strings...You have to start somewhere.

Tune the first of the unison strings to the D above middle C, or to any note you like, until the string is fairly taut and you can play it without it sounding watery. It should be a reasonably high note, and we'll call this note—X. Now tune the second string of the unisons to this first string. Try to get it very close if not exactly the same. Because this string is to be the same as the first, it's X too.

Next, count four frets up the scale beginning with the first fret nearest the nut—large space, large space, small space, large space—and to the left of the fourth fret, about an eighth of an inch in back of the fret, depress the unison strings with the middle finger of your left hand.

With the index finger of your right hand pluck the fretted unisons. The tone you hear is that to which you want to tune the middle string, but you want to tune the middle string an octave lower than the note you produce when you fret the unisons on the fourth fret.

When you fret the unisons on the fourth fret, you produce the fifth tone. Our notation for tuning the middle string to this fifth tone is X+4, and because the middle string is to be an octave-fifth lower than the unisons, we circle the notation. Thus, (X+4) is the notation for tuning the middle string.

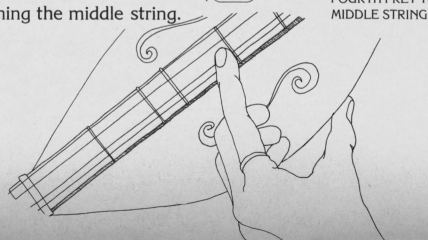

FRETTING THE UNISONS AT THE FOURTH FRET TO TUNE THE MIDDLE STRING

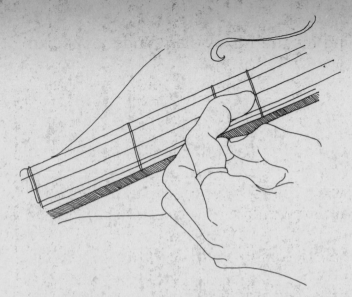

CHECKING THE MIDDLE STRING

To check if you have correctly tuned the middle string, fret it on the third fret (the small spaced one.) Pressing down firmly, pluck it and then the unison strings. You should get almost the same tone from both the middle and unison strings. If not, you haven't gotten the middle string tuned to the octave-fifth value, so keep on trying to get it. Even when the middle note is in tune at the octave-fifth value, its note when fretted on the third fret is not going to be exactly the same as the open unisons. This is because the middle string is thicker than the unisons and produces a different "sound color."

Finally, tune the bass string to an octave below the open unisons. We notate the tuning for the bass string by simply circling (X), indicating an <u>octave below</u> the open X strings. To check your bass string, fret it on the fourth fret and pluck it. It should produce a note the same as the middle string, taking into consideration the differences in sound color.

CHECKING THE BASS STRING

So the tuning for the Mixolydian mode looks like this:

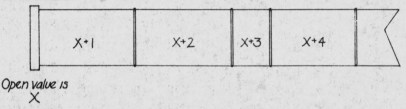

Always read the notation from bottom to top as if you were holding the dulcimer with the headstock to your left.

Each fret has a tuning value, as shown in this illustration.

| X+1 | X+2 | X+3 | X+4 |

Open value is
X

In brief, our tuning procedure for all modes is:

1. Tune the "X" strings (the unisons) first.
2. Always tune to octave values.
3. Always tune the middle and bass strings to the unison strings fretted at the appropriate tuning intervals (X+1, X+2, etc.), depending on into what mode you wish to tune.

If everything's gone well, you should now be tuned into the Mixolydian mode, transposed somewhere, we hope, around the note D. But in any case, the first note of your scale, the "do" note, is the unison note, and the chord you hear when you strike all of the strings should be a pleasant-sounding chord.

When tuning any instrument, you are dealing with tight measurements of sound, tuning tolerances as fine as hundreds of cycles per second and maybe less. And to tune correctly you have to pick these sounds out of the air as they go by. In the beginning, you obviously are not going to get them right all the time. You will get close, but even then what you are hearing and what you think you are hearing are going to be different, especially when you are dealing with the unison strings.

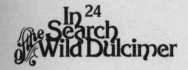

You can possibly alleviate some of the frustration caused by notes being "not quite right" by considering what goes on when you listen. Assume we want to tune the unisons to the D above the middle C on the piano. We already know that D above middle C is rated at 294 cycles per second. Let's say you get one of the unisons to what could be measured at 300 cycles per second, and the other one sounds just about right when you get it to, say, 291. What your ear then registers on your brain is a frequency of 300 cycles per second, one of 291, the difference between the two or nine cycles per second, and the total of the two—591.

So four things are actually happening. When you crawl down into it, you also realize that there is a wavering frequency which blends the notes together —although it's hard to isolate.

One final thing…When you pluck a string too forcefully, you stretch the frequency of its sound by another five or ten cycles per second. So after you think you have your strings tuned, you may have to go back and temper them so that they blend properly, although each may have been all right by itself. And if you are dealing with new strings, you'll have to adjust their tuning regularly for the first day or so until they "break in." Don't be upset if your strings seem to go out of tune almost immediately. They will stabilize.

If you are not yet tuned…relax. You have been bombarding your ears, chasing down sounds you're not used to finding, and you may have rendered yourself temporarily tone deaf.

Tuning is something for which you have to get in shape. Many of the world's best musicians sometimes find it hard to tune, so give yourself a break.

Go for a walk.

Listen to some music.

Do something entirely different.

And then come back to tuning.

We can both remember hours of trying to tune

which finally, mercifully, ended when we broke the strings for which we had no replacements. Then the dulcimer would stand in a corner for days while we sulked and bemoaned a lack of musical talent and a tin ear—all part of a nice, handy, neat and clean prepackaged set of ready-made defeatist attitudes.

No doubt you'll get tuning down in no time at all.

3
Holding and Rhythm and Holding a Rhythm

In 28
the Search
of the Wild Dulcimer

There are many different ways to hold a dulcimer while playing, and an even greater number of ways to hold it if you are not.

We play the dulcimer in a "guitar style"; that is, we attach a strap to each end of the instrument and play standing up with the frets vertical and the dulcimer on its side, hanging across the body horizontally. This method allows for the greatest playing versatility and freedom of movement. You can play sitting down or standing up or dancing with the tune, while still keeping the instrument anchored. This method also puts you in a relationship to the instrument that utilizes a natural "hinge and muscle" arrangement that makes strumming easier.

You'll probably want to start playing sitting down with the dulcimer held sideways across you like a guitar, with the strap over your left shoulder and angling down off your right. It's going to be uncomfort-

able at first, since you weren't born with a piece of wood dangling around your neck, but it will come in no time.

Traditionally, you play the dulcimer while sitting on a low chair, stool or log. The instrument lies across your lap, fretboard side up, with the tuning pegs to your left. Some people find it easier to angle the instrument slightly away from them on the left.

We find the most comfortable sitting position is the yogic style. Sit on the floor with your feet tucked back out of the way and the instrument angling down and off your lap, again with the headstock to your left. This method is a sit-down version of the guitar style—instead of wearing the strap around your shoulders, wrap it around your leg to anchor the instrument. This style is an excellent starting position because it helps you to center yourself over the instrument. Sometimes sitting on a soft pillow or

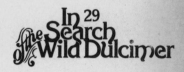

small cushion makes the position more comfortable. Experiment.

In "Autoharp Style" the dulcimer is held vertically with the headstock over your right shoulder. Another twist is to turn it upside down and use the other shoulder. This works well for playing in the front seat of a Volkswagen.

Finally, there's the "Stoval Style," named after Babe Stoval, a truly fine steel guitar blues man from New Orleans. He's not the only one to use this technique, a favorite of superstars for bringing sweating thousands to a final ecstasy. It too is essentially a variation of the guitar style. You swing the instrument up over your head and play it upside down while it rests on your shoulders behind your neck. It's strange, but fun to do, and great for exits.

Later on we'll be discussing picks and picking styles, but for now visit your local music store and buy several light gauge, highly flexible picks which look like this:

If your music store is too far away, or if you are simply into a "resources recycling routine," you can cut up a coffee can lid or bleach bottle and use this plastic material for picks.

You may notice that this "fist pick" is larger than most other picks you've probably seen. It's larger so that your hand can become accustomed to holding this foreign object. Remember when you were in the first grade and began to write with a big, thick, black pencil? Same idea.

Okay. So now you are all set. No more trips to the store for strings, picks, straps, or anything else.

First we're going to work on developing a rhythmic strumming style. We'll be concerned with the tempo (speed) of strumming, the accents within a strummed sequence, and the overall tone of the sound of the rhythm. Then we'll get into playing notes, and notes in sequences, by depressing the unisons to various frets in order to put together melodies. And once we're playing a melody, we'll talk about musical phrases, or passages, which create a total melodic sequence—a song.

And a little later on in the book we'll work on harmonics, picking styles, and finger positions for making melodic chords.

Now, hold your pick any way that is comfortable—between the thumb and forefinger of the right hand is the most usual way. We usually hold it between the thumb and middle finger—keeping the forefinger

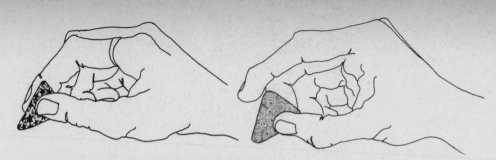

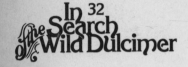

somewhat aloof, bending it down now and then to straighten the pick, which tends to turn during fast tempos.

Rhythm.

Picture yourself sitting around a nicely burning campfire. You shove a protruding stick back into the fire, only to discover that it is already burning underneath and that you have just fried your hand. Your motor senses take over and you start flopping your hand wildly from side to side, up and down, while blowing on it. Notice how the action comes from the wrist.

Great. That's exactly what we want, an up-and-down flopping motion that's very loose at the wrist. It's all in the wrist...Loosen it up...Let it move easily...almost of its own accord. If you can't seem to immediately get it, you're probably trying too hard. Just flop your hand back and forth. Your body knows what to do. Let it happen. If you still can't seem to get it, go on a picnic, and when you find a stick protruding from the fire...

Keep up this side to side flopping motion. Bring your fingers together. Okay...now slow it down a bit. Look at what you're doing, watch your hand, and analyze it.

Now pick up your dulcimer and hold it sideways like a guitar. Get comfortable with it, and then strum.

Down-up/down-up/down-up/down-up/down-up... and so on. Holding the instrument and strumming may prove a bit awkward at first.

Tap your toe each time your hand strums the downbeat. Your toe will be raised for the upbeat. If you really get into it, whomp your whole foot

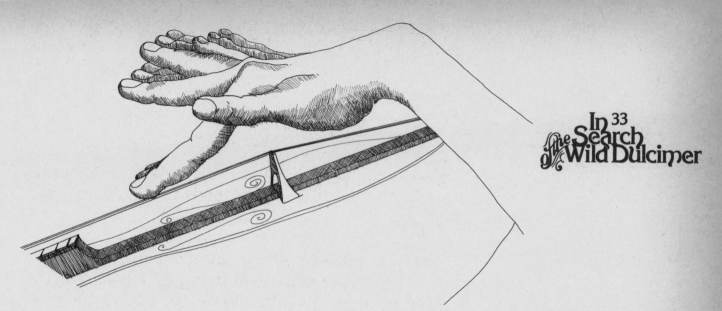

on the floor; but whatever you do, try to keep your down-up strum at an even, non-jerky pace...nice and even, very fluid.

All this is the beginning technique for rhythmic strumming. The dulcimer is a very rhythmic instrument, and we're laying the foundation for your playing. The speed at which you are strumming determines the tempo—no matter how fast or slow it is or whether you are in the process of increasing or diminishing that speed, each one of the divisions (down/up) within the tempo is a beat.

Now lay your left hand on top of the dulcimer near the area around the nut, and with your forefinger or middle finger lightly cross all of the strings just to the right and parallel to the nut. Don't depress the strings, just lay your finger on top of them. This will uniformly <u>mute</u> the strings so that you can better hear your strumming. Holding the pick in your right hand, strum the strings, crossing them perpendicularly about four to six inches from the bridge.

VIEW OF HAND AS IT MOVES THROUGH THE STRUM

TOP VIEW OF RIGHT HAND IN STRUM POSITION

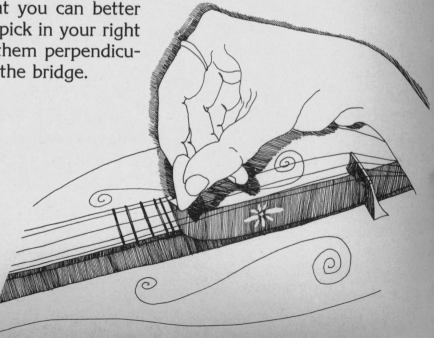

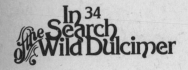

Find a tempo you can keep constant (no matter how slow) and a strum you find easy. It makes sense to practice the basic down-up strum because this strum is the essential aspect of dulcimer playing. Vary it when you want to and practice other strum patterns—like playing all downstrokes and then all upstrokes: down/down/down/down—up/up/up/up—down/down/down/down—up/up/up/up... You might want to try something like down/down/down/up/down—down/down/down/up/down: strum down three times, up once, and down once again, with the third downstroke and the one upstroke each taking half as long as each of the other three strokes: 1, 2, 3-&, 4. Count it out loud.

Get used to the pick hitting the strings. How tightly you hold the pick makes a difference in how much "pick drag" you receive from the strings. Carry a pick with you wherever you go and practice your strumming on the side of a book, table, your leg—anything at all. The purpose now is to strengthen your wrist, get used to the pick, and strike the strings (or any other surface) uniformly and at an even rate.

Do this strumming awhile, keeping the strings muted. Concentrate on your speed and beats. Don't go too fast, keep it steady and even, and look at your right hand because, right now, that's where it's happening.

Now we're going to hear what those strings really sound like. Using the down/down/down—up/down strum sequence, strum the strings, and on the one upstroke, quickly lift the index finger of your left hand which has been muting the strings. Lift this finger only on the upstroke, and get your finger back down to mute the strings in time for the next beat. (It may be like rubbing your stomach and patting your head for the first time.) Timing and the development of ear-hand coordination are important elements of playing music.

Experiment with this. The more you strum and practice the up- and downstrokes, the more you will develop your rhythmic sense. You can make up your own combinations of up and down...but keep your rhythms even and maintain a tempo that is reasonable. And remember—watch your hand when you practice. Be aware.

By now you probably have a sound like down/down/down/"twang"/down. Try lifting your finger on different beats. Or reverse the process: Strum with the strings open and mute whichever beats you want. Either way, notice the emphasis or accent you are giving. Try increasing the force with which you strike the strings on that upbeat without lifting your finger. It's the same effect, but with a little different tone.

Speaking of tone, that's another way to accent. Tone refers to the quality of the sound. We started playing four to six inches up from the bridge, but if you strum closer to the bridge, the tone sharpens until finally, when you are playing almost on top of the bridge itself, you get a very metallic "twanging" sound. The strings are more rigid there and resist vibrating to their fullest capacity.

In strumming, what we're striving for is a lateral swinging motion of the arm and wrist that uses the different sound colors produced by strumming anywhere from right on the bridge to four to six inches up from the bridge, where the tone is very blended and mellow. You probably won't be using this lateral strumming technique immediately, but you might begin exploring the variety of subtle sound colors you can achieve.

Additional tonal quality and string emphasis can be added by changing the angle at which you strike the strings. If you roll your hand slightly toward you as you strum, you get <u>treble</u> (unison string) emphasis; if you roll your hand away from you, emphasizing the bass string, the bass becomes dominant. When using this wrist-roll technique, you bisect the plane of the strings from about a 30-degree angle either way and accent whichever string you want.

Practice your strumming...it's the only way you'll be able to play with a fluidity that will be a part of your music. You first lay down a basic strum. So it

STRUMMING ANGLES

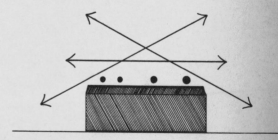

does not become boring or monotonous, vary it with different techniques:

> —how fast or slow you strum
> —which beats you select for accentuation
> —how tightly you hold the pick
> —how strongly you strike the strings
> —where you strum along the fretboard
> —the angle at which you strike the strings
> —when you mute and un-mute the strings

All the elements we've discussed—beats, tempo, tone, accent, string emphasis—are part of what makes up a basic rhythmic playing style, but rhythm itself is greater than the sum of its parts. Rhythm is the cornerstone of music. It is the counting out that marks the passage of time colored in different ways. Even in a-rhythmic playing, it is conspicuous in its absence, for somehow the flow of time has to be marked, whether you choose to dwell within it or not.

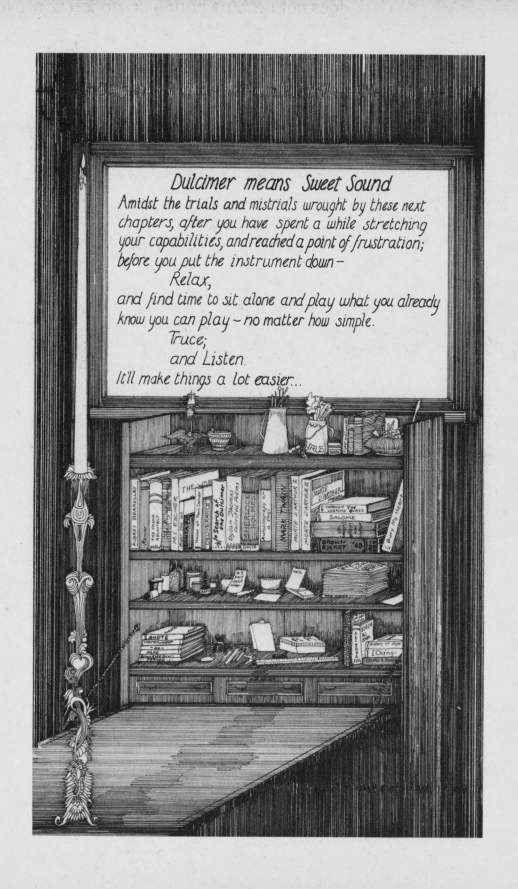

Dulcimer means Sweet Sound

Amidst the trials and mistrials wrought by these next
chapters, after you have spent a while stretching
your capabilities, and reached a point of frustration;
before you put the instrument down –
　　　　Relax,
and find time to sit alone and play what you already
know you can play – no matter how simple.
　　　　Truce;
　　　　and Listen.
It'll make things a lot easier...

4
Melody and the Mixolydian Mode

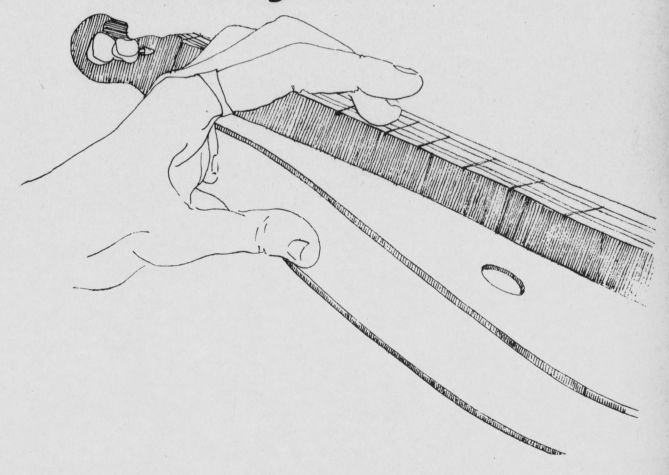

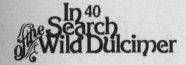

Let's find out what this Mixolydian mode is all about, now that we know how to tune into it and have done some strumming. A _mode_ is a particular arrangement of seven notes plus the repeat. Most modes end on an octave, although some obscure ones end on a fifth or a fourth tone. (These are not used very much, however, except in monastic Gregorian chanting.)

The fret arrangement of the dulcimer is based on the assumption that the first, or open note, is "G." If we play the white notes on a piano between G above middle C and G above high C (G and g, in our illustration), the letter values of the notes played would look like this on a music staff.

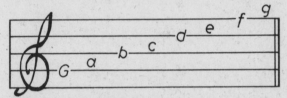

We would have just played a _scale_—a succession of tones and half-tones alphabetically labeled and arranged in ascending or descending order from any given note, or keytone, to its octave tone eight notes away. This is the scale of the Mixolydian mode.

Some people claim that in the sixth century B.C. the mathematician Pythagoras, by means of a single vibrating string called "monochord," established the mathematical ratios of the scale which has been the basis of music in the West. The chart (on p.41) from an early seventeeth-century German physics book portrays one conception of the diatonic scale.

But whatever the history, if you refer the letter values of the Mixolydian mode to the dulcimer's diatonic fretboard, you can plainly see that each of the frets carries a note value going up the scale. It's also obvious that the spaces between the frets "b-c" and "e-f" are proportionately smaller than the spaces between the other frets.

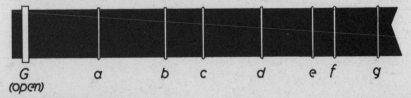

G   a   b   c   d   e f   g
(open)

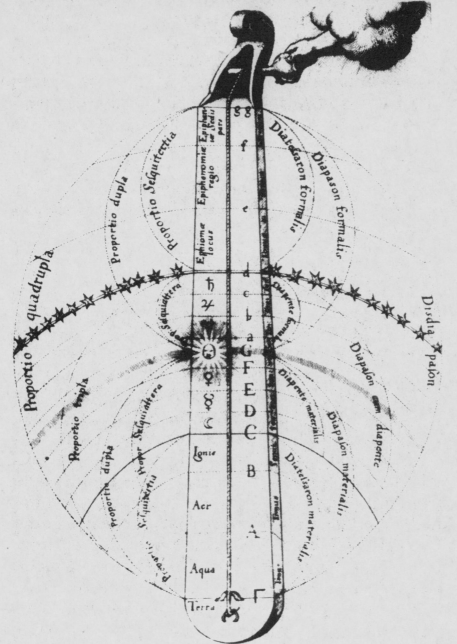

Whenever you sing or play the standard "major" scale (do-re-mi-fa-sol-la-ti-do), each of the notes sounds tonally equidistant. They sound "whole" or "perfect" in and of themselves, as well as in their tonal sequence. Over the centuries our ears have become accustomed to this scale, and we think it sounds perfect—and perhaps it does. But it really isn't "perfect." This common major scale actually consists of six "whole tones" and two "half-tones"—not eight whole tones as it sounds.

In this common major scale (played on eight consecutive white notes on the piano, beginning on the note C), the half-tones are the intervals between the notes "mi" and "fa" and "ti" and "do"—positions 3 and 4, and 7 and 8. But on the dulcimer's scale the half-tones are between "mi and fa" and "la and ti"—that is, positions 3 and 4, and 6 and 7. This particular arrangement corresponds to the notes b and c, and e and f exactly as shown in illustration 38. Indeed, the half-tones of the common major scale fall between the same notes, but <u>where</u> the notes are in relation to the other notes (what the sequence is) is different from that of the dulcimer's scale.

In the case of the dulcimer's fret scale, the "particular arrangement" of the eight tones is referred to as a "<u>fixed scheme</u>" in that the intervals between the notes fall into a never-varying, universally accepted pattern. This concept of <u>fixed schemes</u> is fundamental to the dulcimer's modal tuning system, so keep it in mind as we go along...It's all in the <u>schemes.</u>

The phenomenon of half-steps occurs because people began singing modes before they began writing them down. When people started writing music, it was for instruments like the harp, psaltery, and lyre that had individual strings for each of the notes, so the inconsistency of the two half-notes wasn't apparent. But when people began making and playing fretted instruments, they discovered rather quickly that they had to justify these tonal inconsistencies, and they did so by developing the idea of fixed modal schemes.

Every modal scale has a different arrangement of these two half-tones within the structure of the six whole tones. The <u>tonal</u> scheme of the Mixolydian mode, then, is: whole tone/ whole tone/ whole tone/ half tone/ whole tone/ whole tone/ half tone/ whole tone, which then repeats as the scale moves into higher octaves. A more concise way of writing a mode's fixed scheme is to count the intervals between the notes themselves. For the Mixolydian mode the interval scheme is: whole step/ whole step/ half step/ whole step/ whole step/ half step/ whole step, or: 1—1—½—1—1—½—1—seven intervals between eight notes.

As you can see, the scheme of the Mixolydian mode is identical to the usual fret arrangement of the dulcimer. To begin the scale at G is as seemingly arbitrary as beginning at any other note. Nonetheless, this is historically where the dulcimer's scale arrangement was figured from for the sake of standardization and reference, and it does place middle C exactly there—in the middle (GAB<u>C</u>DEF).

Since we all have to use this particular scale concept and method for applying letter values, you will have to remember along with everyone else involved with music in the Western world, that the b—c and e—f intervals are <u>half-tones.</u> It's just that simple. (It is here that so many people drop out of music because, really, it doesn't make much sense at all, except historically.)

Now, of course you don't have to be at the vibrational frequency known as the note G to be tuned to the Mixolydian mode—we've already found this to be true. You know you can tune to anything your strings and ears will tolerate as long as your strongest, or <u>tonic</u>, note is on the open strum. It is the relationship between strings that is important, not the actual notes themselves. Likewise, it is the relation of the steps of the scale to one another in the fixed scheme of 1—1—½—1—1—½—1 which determines whether or not you are in the Mixolydian mode.

If you actually happen to be at the open chord value of G (which may be a bit too high for unison strings of the .010 gauge), that's wonderful. You can then tell people you are tuned in the traditional Mixolydian mode. If your unisons are pitched someplace else, your tuning is <u>transposed</u>.

Using D as our keytone, the letter values for each note going up the scale when tuned into the Mixolydian mode are:

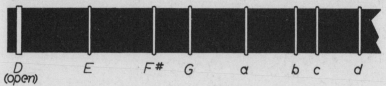

D E F# G a b c d
(open)

Now we're ready for melody, and you may even have learned a little history, some music theory, and a few terms in getting here.

Okay...Music gotta' have feet. But before beginning this section on melody, sit and drum the fingers of your left hand on something. Drum... drum...drum...That's just the motion you want to use to fret the unisons. For playing melodies on the dulcimer, your forefinger and middle finger will become your most valuable tools. Later, we'll use additional fingers to add effects and flourishes, and to make chords. Also, we'll discuss techniques for fretting with other objects.

For now, we are going to fret with the tip of the middle finger of the left hand on both of the two melody or unison strings. Unlike the position used in playing a guitar or banjo, your left hand should come over the top of the instrument, not up onto the strings from the bottom.

As we go along, you will find that certain notes on our scale link into patterns. The first pattern is a four-note sequence: Octave (open)-third-fifth-midoctave. Another way to describe this is: Open strum-second fret-fourth fret-seventh fret. To make things even easier, let's number the notes of the first octave on the fretboard. The open note will be one, the first fretted note will be two, and so on up to eight. The first sequence will now read 1—3—5—8. (There are three notes between 1 and 3, hence the term third; and five notes between 1 and 5, hence fifth.) This 1—3—5 pattern is basic to a major chordal structure; that is, the third and fifth tones complement or harmonize with the open or root tone. So when we play this kind of a melodic sequence, all we're really doing is playing note elements of a major chord.

The next series of linked notes are frets 2—4—6. Put them all together and try playing something like this:

1 — 3 — 5 — 8
1 — 3 — 5 — 8
2 — 4 — 6 — pause
2 — 4 — 6 — pause
1 — 3 — 5 — 8
1 — 3 — 5 — 8

When fretting, try to slide your middle finger from fret to fret without lifting it off the fretboard except to voice the open note. Practice this with various combinations of up- and downstrokes. If you can't find a rhythmic pattern that lends itself to down/up strumming, start by using all downstrokes.

By exercising these patterns up and down the scale, you will learn where the notes are on the fretboard. Later, when we get into the other modes, this same kind of sequential exercise will help you familiarize yourself with the tonal relationships unique to each mode.

Most likely you have been playing a four-beat sequence with a rest instead of a played beat during the 2—4—6 <u>measure.</u> Instead of resting there, why not add another 6. So this part now reads 2—4—6—6 ...and so on.

Now we'll add the seventh tone. In the Mixolydian mode it sounds rather <u>minor</u> or mournful in relation to the other notes. Generally, the sound of a minor note dictates a change in your rhythmic pattern; the Mixolydian's slightly dissonant seventh tone blends differently and demands such a change. Each of the other notes is getting just one beat per measure (except for the two sixes) but the seventh demands several. Even when you give the seventh more beats, it still sounds too "weak" to stand alone. It needs something—another note—to "complete" it. Its dissonance must be resolved to consonance. So try this:

$$1 - 3 - 5 - 8$$
$$1 - 3 - 5 - 8$$
$$2 - 4 - 6 - 6$$
$$2 - 4 - 6 - 6$$
$$1 - 3 - 5 - 8$$
$$1 - 3 - 5 - 8$$
$$7 - 7 - 7 - 7$$
$$7 - 7 - 7 - 8$$

Now the seventh sounds completed. The entire sequence has been resolved and here, in part, lies the essence of a <u>phrase</u>—a musical segment or statement that is completed upon reaching the resolve.

We have been giving each of these notes a whole beat every time we play it. As you get faster and more proficient in your coordination, you may want to begin splitting the value of your beats. You can split them in half, then again into quarters, into eighths, sixteenths, thirty-seconds, sixty-fourths... The master violinist Paginini did some truly incredible things beyond that.

A simple notation for dividing beats is a slash mark (/). This notation means that you play the note on either side of the line twice as fast as a whole beat. So try this sequence:

$$1 - 3 - 5/5 - 8$$
$$1 - 3 - 5/5 - 8$$
$$2 - 4 - 6/6 - 6$$
$$2 - 4 - 6/6 - 6$$
$$1 - 3 - 5/5 - 8$$
$$1 - 3 - 5/5 - 8$$
$$7 - 7 - 7 - 7$$
$$7 - 7 - 7 - 8$$

A variety of strumming strokes can be used with this sequence. One with which it might be good to start is a series of all downstrokes (or upstrokes) except for the half-time notation where a down/up strum stroke cuts the beat in half.

If you find sliding one finger through all these changes to be a little awkward, you are no doubt more than ready for the two-finger technique which utilizes both the middle and index fingers. Place your middle finger at the octave fret and slide down the scale playing each note as you go, then come back up the scale by using your index finger to depress each note. Thus, for moving around the fretboard use the middle finger to move downward, and the index finger for upward movement. Additionally, the middle finger is easily used to hold down a note as a "base" while the index finger reaches out to play other notes in rapid succession.

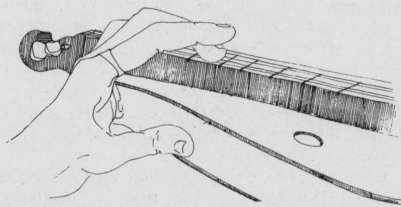

TWO-FINGER FRETTING TECHNIQUE

Try this: first strum the open note, and while it is still sounding, quickly put your middle finger down at the first fret. Strum this note, and while it is still sounding depress the next fret with your index finger. Then, lifting your index finger up off the note, slide the middle finger to the fret your index finger just got off of, and sound that note. Repeat this depress-and-slide technique all the way up the scale. By reversing the process, do it all the way back to the open note.

Work with the elements and techniques we have talked about. Get into the habit of depressing the unison strings firmly, maximizing the tone you pro-

duce. Practice using both fingers. Experiment with the notes, note sequences, beats and fingerings. Make up your own melodies, and remember that the sequence of upstrokes, downstrokes, and down/up strokes depends on the formation of the melody you are playing—where the notes occur in the melody in relation to the rhythm.

And songs? Well, some fine, basic songs to work with and improvise around are songs of your childhood like "Frère Jacques," "Twinkle, Twinkle, Little Star," "This Old Man, He Played One," "London Bridge Is Falling Down," "She'll Be Comin' 'Round the Mountain," "Go Tell Aunt Rhody," "Oh Susanna!" "You Are My Sunshine," "Down in the Valley," "Old Joe Clark" (which is unique to the Mixolydian mode), "Cripple Creek," "Wildwood Flower," "Banks of the Ohio," and one of our favorites, "Boil Them Cabbage Down, Boys!"

Play what you know. If you don't know any songs at all, make some up. That's the point of all this anyway. If you have trouble picking out a tune and finding the notes "by ear," we've listed some music books in Chapter XI ("Some Useful Charts, Books, and Records of Interest") that give you simple songs to play.

A good exercise game consists of playing children's songs like "Twinkle, Twinkle, Little Star," "Frère Jacques," "This Old Man," and "London Bridge" all together. As you get to a point in one song that has the same beginning note as a phrase you recognize in another song, switch songs and maybe even rhythms. Doing this will show you not only how songs are put together but also how they come apart. It will make you think ahead to what you are going to do next, and how that relates to what you are doing at the moment and what you have already done.

Here's an example—and it may help a little if you sing this through a couple of times to get into what's happening:

"This old man, he played one,
He played knick-knack on my drum,
With a

Twinkle, twinkle, little star,
How I wonder what you

Frère Jacques,
Frère Jacques,
Dormez-vous?
Dormez-vous?

London Bridge is falling down,
Falling down, falling down,

With a knick-knack, patty-wack,
Give a dog a bone,
This old man is going home..."

And so on.

This same system can be used with increasingly difficult songs; then again, by the time you are playing more difficult songs, you won't need games.

The Mixolydian mode is the easiest and most straightforward mode to learn with because it forgives much more readily than its fellows—you can always fall back upon the open strum to gain the "breather" you might need from time to time while playing.

So we'll stay with the Mixolydian for one more section and take a look at different techniques for embellishing the melody line.

5
Odds
and Ends
of Technique

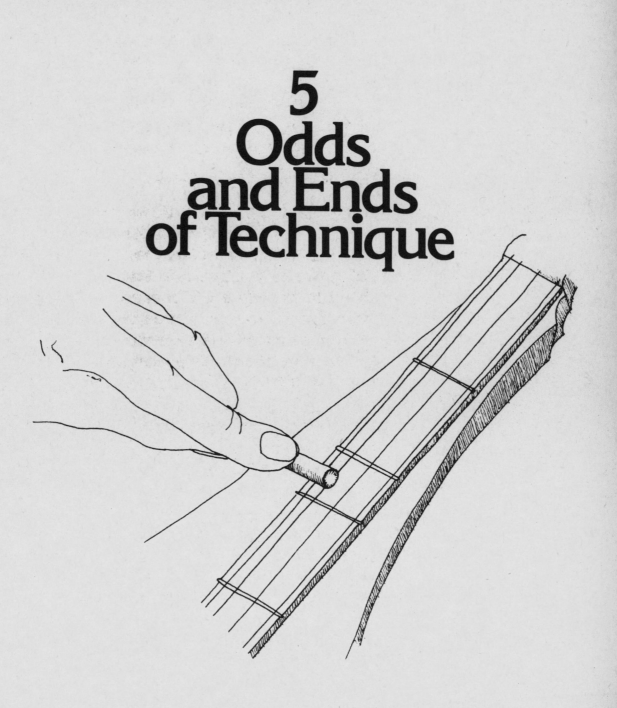

The techniques we are going to discuss are only a few of the many that can conceivably be used on the dulcimer; however, we hope to describe them in a way that not only will be clear but that will also prompt you to think of your own ways of playing.

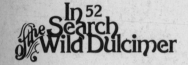

HAMMERING ON AND PULLING OFF

If while using the two-finger technique with your left hand, you bring your index finger down sharply and forcefully onto the strings, the action of quickly driving the string down to the fretboard will cause the tone to voice even before the rhythm hand catches that particular note with a strum. Think of your finger as a hammer hitting the string and re-coiling as quickly as possible.

For "pulling off," you "twang" the string with the left hand, that is, after applying the pressure on the string to make the note, you then pull your finger off the string and toward you.

You can practice both these techniques by playing melodies with the left hand alone. The only vibration the strings will receive is hammering and pulling off.

A "riff" we practice is the phrase before the cannons fire in Tchaikovsky's "1812 Overture." This nine-note phrase can be played completely by hammering on and pulling off with the fingers of the left hand.

TRIPLETS

When you play a triplet series, you are squeezing three notes into one beat. To play triplets, you can use the ring finger as a base. First hammer onto the fretboard with the ring finger, and then follow it in quick succession onto the next frets with the middle finger and then the forefinger. Reversing the process, have all of these fingers on the fretboard, each covering an individual note. Starting with the forefinger, pull each of them off in rapid succession.

This can take a little practice.

WAVERS AND
QUAVERS (TREMOLO)

When you are playing a note and want to "schmaltz" it up a bit to make it sound romantic, melancholic or forlorn, all you have to do is move your finger back and forth quickly on the spot where you are depressing the string. Don't change the position of your finger; rather, just move it quickly from side to side as if you were pressing and gluing something there. Remember not to let up on the pressure.

INDIVIDUAL STRING
PLAYING

So far you have been playing only the first two strings, the unisons. You already know that the bass string is tuned an octave below your unisons, so you should have no trouble applying the fretting techniques you have learned to the fourth string. The only thing you may have to learn to do is arch your fingers a little more so that you don't dampen the other strings as you reach over them. Try playing on the bass string if you haven't already done so.

In the Mixolydian mode the middle string is tuned to a fifth of the melody strings. To play a simple scale on the middle string, start at the third fret (the first half-tone fret) and play the scale up to the octave, which should be on the tenth fret. You'll notice that this scale doesn't have the "odd" sounding seventh tone. As a matter of fact, it's the standard fixed scheme of the Ionian mode.

In the Mixolydian, the seventh tone of the first octave (the note we find to be so minor) is not a "true" seventh; instead, it's a sharpened sixth (or, enharmonically, a flatted 7th.) In the Ionian, it is a true or natural seventh; however, if, while playing in the Mixolydian, you use the seventh tone of the middle string's first octave (found on the tenth fret) you will be "breaking" the <u>modality</u> of the Mixolydian, and this natural seventh will sound out of place when

strummed. It's like having the "extra fret" we spoke about in the section on tuning.

You can play melodies on the middle string, but the tune may not stand out over the drone of the unisons and the bass. By lessening the arch of your left hand fingers and allowing them to lightly touch the unisons, you can effectively dampen the unisons whenever you don't want them overpowering the quiet middle string. Nonetheless, the effect is very mellow, and has a certain subtlety. The middle string also makes it possible for you to play the ever-popular "shave-and-a-haircut, two-bits" ending.

By separately fretting each of the unisons on frets one fret-space apart, you can play minor thirds. To do this, push the inside string (second string) away from you with your middle finger to widen the gap between it and the first string. With your index finger, pull the outside unison string toward you. If you are depressing each of these strings on two different frets, one space apart, you should get the desired sound.

HARMONICS

These are the bell-like tones you produce when you rest your finger ever-so-lightly across the strings at points which divide the string length into equal portions. The distance from the nut to the bridge should be exactly twice as long as the distance from the nut to where your eighth tone, or first octave note, is.

Without depressing the strings, lay your forefinger across the strings over the first octave fret. You should be touching so lightly that you can barely feel the strings. Now, strum rapidly and very briskly with the pick, and as you do, quickly lift your finger off the strings. You should produce a bell-tone, a chime. If you didn't, try it again…and again. It is there, and you'll get it shortly.

You know that this first harmonic, the strongest

of all the harmonic notes, is at the midpoint of the instrument. There is only one harmonic of this particular tone; the other harmonics come in sets of two. What you find at half the distance between the nut and the first harmonic, you will also find at the same distance between the first harmonic and the bridge. Thus, your second harmonics are found over both the fourth and eleventh frets. The third harmonics are over the second and sixteenth frets. Actually, there is a harmonic tone over each fret, if it has been placed accurately; however, these can be difficult to find and hard to hear once you have found them. Harmonics make good endings, bringing the rhythm and melody to a quick close. They can also be used as accents within rhythms.

USE OF THE NOTER

The noter, sometimes called a "fretter" or "playing stick," is a finger-length cylindrical piece of wood about a quarter of an inch thick. It is used most often by traditional dulcimer players who hold it as if it were an extra finger, usually between the thumb and index finger. To depress the unison strings, you run the noter up and down the fretboard, and as you play it makes a slight "whistling" noise.

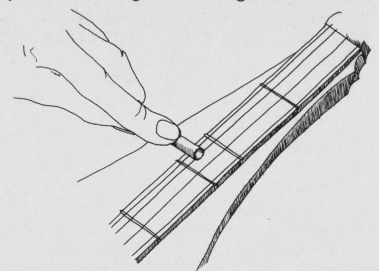

TRADITIONAL USE OF THE NOTER

There are drawbacks to using the noter, although the effect is quite pleasing, and one of these is that you have minimal contact with the strings, and therefore limited string control.

One interesting technique employs a noter made of slippery surfaced "wet" plastic. While playing a song, quickly move the noter off the strings and insert it underneath the melody strings at the cutaway portion of the fretboard. Then slide it back to the area where the melody was being played. This is like having a movable nut and creates a "blues" sound. Also, you can depress the strings behind the noter with your middle finger, and make the tone waver up a half-step or more. This sounds very much like a "Bottleneck" guitar.

SLIDING THE NOTER UNDER THE UNISON STRINGS

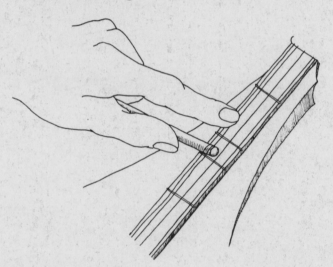

BENDING NOTES

Bending notes resembles the technique of separating the melody strings to play thirds, but in this case you simply move the string slightly with your fingertip while it is depressed to the fret in order to alter its tone. You "bend" the note's sound to make its tone climb a maximum of a half-tone or so. Again, strictly speaking, doing this takes you out of mode, but a well-placed bent note can add a great deal to a melodic passage. One thing to watch out for is the elusiveness of the melody strings when you're bending both of them—they can wiggle out from beneath your fingertip easily, so make sure you are using enough downward pressure to stabilize their movement.

PLAYING NOTES WHICH AREN'T THERE

Eventually you will want to play a song which has one or more notes that are not included in your scale. There are four ways to get around this problem.

1 You can bend the note on the fret <u>below</u> the one you want and make it a half-step higher. Since you are going for an exact tone, this will be difficult until you learn to gauge how much the string should be bent to produce the desired note.

2 Rarely, but sometimes, you can get the note you want by using the harmonics of the instrument; however, this can sound a bit out of place.

3 You can make a change in the rhythm and leave the note out entirely. Here, you don't actually produce the note, but the listener will fill it in. Also, in the time/beat space allowed for that note, you can slide around it by playing the notes just below and above it, "passing through" the note without really playing it.

4 This method is really part of the next section, but you can always change the tuning to a different mode. You will probably find the note you are looking for, but then again you may lose a few of the other notes you need. Most songs that are "major" in mood can be played in either the Mixolydian or Ionian modes, and the Ionian comes next.

While learning to play the dulcimer, don't forget that the most important thing you can do is to improve your strumming and your sense of rhythm. The more you play, the more fluid your strum will

become, and the better, quicker, and more sensitive you will be.

You've undoubtedly found that it doesn't take a great deal of strength or effort to produce sound on the dulcimer. Often, too much pressure in strumming ruins the otherwise pleasing, delicate sounds your instrument can create. <u>Listen</u> to what you are playing.

<u>Syncopation</u>—the changing around of beats and their accents—will enhance your playing, making your rhythms more varied, interesting and altogether different in impact.

Nothing is constant!

Change it around.

Use two or three fingering methods in any given song. Do what sounds good to you—even rewrite the tune if you want to. Few listeners will miss the notes, and maybe our song will be more pleasing than the original. Who knows?

Drop beats, make it "funky." Even "Go Tell Aunt Rhody" can really cook if you get into it.

Whatever you do though, make sure that your embellishments and finger techniques are not cover-ups for poor strumming and non-rhythms. No left-hand technique can make up for a right hand that is not doing its job.

6
Five
More
Modes

Besides the Mixolydian mode, there are six other modern modes. We'll get into five of them in this section, and we'll take up the seventh one, the Locrian, later.

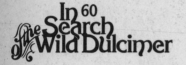

THE IONIAN MODE— TRADITIONAL FOLK TUNING

In our notation, the Ionian mode's tuning is like this:

$$\begin{array}{c} \textcircled{X} \\ \underline{\textcircled{X+3}} \\ X \\ X \end{array}$$

The first note of the scale begins on the third fret of the unisons, where the mode's most major-sounding tonality is found. The Ionian mode originally began at the note C on the third fret. Its scheme is $1-1-\frac{1}{2}-1-1-1-\frac{1}{2}$.

Many folk songs use the Ionian tuning because it is the standard major scale. The mode contains eight "perfect to the ear" intervals, and a natural seventh tone replaces the Mixolydian's minor seventh. From the scheme of the Ionian and its eight perfect tones, the chromatic major scales took form. Over the course of many years, each of the modal fixed schemes underwent half-tone alterations to make it conform to the relative tonalities of the Ionian mode. The minor seventh of the Mixolydian was replaced with an F-sharp, thereby creating the G-major scale out of the G-mode.

You can play most major-sounding songs in the Ionian mode, and in many cases they will be the same ones you play in the Mixolydian. From our standpoint, the Ionian's only drawback is the loss of the open strum, but since you gain the natural seventh tone, things balance out. Because the Ionian is the traditional dulcimer major tuning, many players tune to its original keytone, C. In notation this tuning looks like this (given that X is G):

$(X+3)$
X
X
X

As you know, tuning your .010 unisons up to G may break them, so if you are going to use this traditional tuning a great deal, you'd best get slightly thinner (.009 gauge) extra-light strings. If you tune your unisons down to a G below middle C on the piano, use two .012's for unisons, as well as for the middle string.

Once again, the first note of your scale is at the third fret, and in this tuning your third fret actually will be C. The middle string will be C, and the bass will be an octave below G.

Some people tune the Ionian mode with all the strings the same, and the effect is quite pleasing for Scotch, English, or Irish ballads that require a strong bagpipe-like drone behind the melody line. This tuning looks like this:

X
X
X
X

If you are tuned into the Mixolydian mode with D as your keytone for the unisons, you will automatically be in the key of G when you lower your middle string one note to tune into the Ionian. This is handy when you are playing with other musicians who like the key of G.

There are literally hundreds if not thousands of Irish, Scottish, English, French, German, Scandinavian and certainly American folk songs that you can play in the Ionian mode. We recommend Jean Ritchie's and Lynn McSpadden's dulcimer books as two of many that contain songs written in music tablature that is easy to understand. At the back of this book you'll find a listing of these and other titles.

AEOLIAN—THE MAJOR MINOR

The Aeolian mode is the old A-minor mode—"A" because this note is its historical keytone; "minor," because of the nature of its scale, which follows the scheme 1—½—1—1—½—1—1. If you read the Aeolian's fixed scheme backward, you'll see it is the reverse of the Mixolydian. The Aeolian is the most forceful of all the minor modes. The first note of the Aeolian's scale begins on the first fret, and the tuning is like this:

$$\boxed{X+1}$$
$$\boxed{X+5}$$
$$X$$
$$X$$

The Aeolian is minor because the third note in its scale forms a minor third with the keytone. The Aeolian has a minor sixth, too, and its melancholic tone lends itself to creative, lyrical phrasing.

Its drawbacks stem from the nature of its minor tonality. Open strumming produces a disquieting "when-is-the-second-shoe-going-to-drop?" feeling that demands resolution. Many of the notes in the scale have this same effect. Playing notes on the middle and bass strings becomes strange, since you no longer have major tone drones behind the unisons. To play on the middle or bass string, you must be careful to play each string by itself, because they do not blend with the unisons.

Some tunes you can play in the Aeolian are "Shady Grove," "Charlie's Sweet," "John Henry," "The Cuckoo," Richard Fariña's "The Falcon," "Cluck Old Hen," "God Rest Ye Merry, Gentlemen" and some of your favorite blues songs.

THE DORIAN MODE

Originally tuned to D, the Dorian has a slightly major-sounding tonality but is considered a minor mode. The Dorian is used in traditional folk music more often than the Aeolian because it is very easy to tune from the major Ionian to the minor Dorian.

The first note of the Dorian's scale falls on the fourth fret and follows the scheme 1—½—1—1—1—½—1. Its tuning is:

(X+1)
(X+4)
X
X

Playing on the middle and bass strings works well in the Dorian, especially on the bass string, with the sixth fret as a keytone. At times you may hit notes reminiscent of a merry-go-round slightly out of whack, but when we get into chording, remember the Dorian.

You generally can play the same songs in the Dorian mode as in the Aeolian, but of course you start at a different place. The Dorian has an altogether different "feel," and is excellent when the music doesn't demand a strong minor like the Aeolian. Transposing songs from one mode to another will acquaint you with many of the modes' scales.

THE PHRYGIAN MODE

You may find it difficult to tune into this mode when your unisons are pitched around D because your bass string may break. You might want to tune all the strings down a step or so to somewhere around C. If you are in doubt as to whether your strings can handle tuning into Phrygian without lowering everything, check in the back of the book and get acquainted with the Range and Tuning Guide.

The fixed scheme of this mode is ½—1—1—1—½—1—1. Its original keytone was E, and the notation is:

(X+2)
(X+5)
X
X

The scale begins at the fifth fret, and it is a very hauntingly minor mode. At least one murder ballad is played in the Phrygian ("Pretty Polly") and blues can be played in it, too.

THE LYDIAN MODE

Originally the F-mode, the Lydian was very popular in Renaissance times with wandering troubadors. The Lydian begins on the sixth fret, and its scheme is 1—1—1—½—1—1—½. The tuning notation is:

$\boxed{X+6}$ (double octave)
$\boxed{X+3}$
X
X

Once again, to avoid breaking strings, lower the pitch of the dulcimer one or two notes to a C or a B. Don't let the double octave notation throw you—it's not particularly hard to do. When you think it through, you'll find the Lydian's bass string is only one note below where it would be in an Ionian tuning. To check the bass, fret the unisons on the first fret and the bass on the second—you should get the same note an octave apart.

Except for a very strange, minor fourth tone of the octave, the Lydian could be another Ionian. The development of these two modes and the addition of a B-flat note was part of the rapid advance of <u>harmony</u> that occurred in music in the early sixteenth century. Any tunes you can play in the Ionian that don't require the fourth tone of the scale will adapt to Lydian tuning. Some basic songs are "Cripple Creek," "Little Liza Jane," and "Shortnin' Bread."

So here are five more modes. Each one has its own very special "mood," so take time to listen to each of them. What feelings does each of them evoke within you?

7
Pickin'

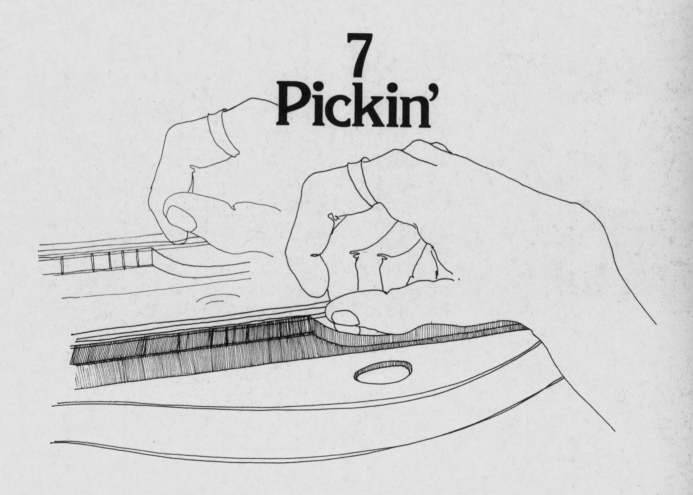

Pickin' can be broken down into four separate styles:

1 Strumming
2 Flat-pickin'
3 Finger-pickin'
4 Beating, Scraping, Banging, and Other Specialty Styles

We've already started with strumming. To further your strumming techniques, try different kinds of picks—different thicknesses, shapes, or materials, such as felt, tortoise shell, whittled wood, or "Appalachian style" with the quill end of a goose feather.

In this section, we're going to concern ourselves with the three other kinds of pickin'.

FLAT-PICKIN'

To flat-pick, you strike the individual strings within different rhythmic schemes. The pick is held as if for strumming; however, the motion comes entirely from the wrist, with the pick descending in small arcs to pluck each individual string according to the sequence.

For example, call the unison strings "position one," the middle string "position two," and the bass "position three." A simple flat-picking sequence is like this:

1 — 3 — 1 — 2
1 — 3 — 1 — 2
1 — 3 — 1 — 2
1 — 3 — 1 — 2…and so on

The "one" stroke is picked away from you and the "two" and "three" strokes are picked toward you so that you achieve a fluid motion and maintain a rhythm. Another common practice sequence is:

1 — 1 — 3
1 — 1 — 3
1 — 2 — 1 — 2 — 1 — 2 — 3…and so on

There are many different patterns for flat-picking. Anything's fair. If you are in doubt, remember that no matter what the sequence, if you do it at least twice in a row, it will work.

FINGER-PICKIN'

We group a great deal under this heading, believing that if you pick specifically with your fingers, then that's what it is. Some people grow their fingernails a little longer on the pickin' hand, but most people's nails are too soft for continuous use as picks. You might purchase a set of steel or plastic finger-picks. Finger-picks fit over the ends of your fingers and act as fingernails so you can pluck the strings in rapid succession without suffering blisters or having to build up callouses.

As with flat-picking, finger-picking sequences are many and varied, but any sequences you can do with a flat pick can be done with your finger-picks. Moreover, with finger picks you can use the thumb to "double strum" between the unisons and middle or bass string to syncopate the rhythm.

ONE FINGER

But let's start with one finger.

You can use any one finger (usually the forefinger and sometimes the thumb) in a flat-picking style. Also, try brushing one finger across the strings from the bass to treble at an angle. Staying on the same plane as the strings and brushing lightly gives you a whistling bagpipe sound.

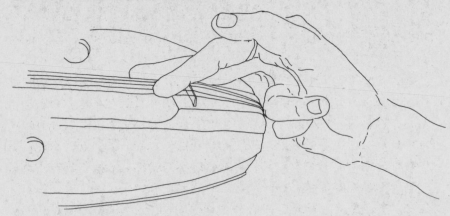

BRUSHING THE STRINGS WITH THE
INDEX FINGER

You can also rest your hand against the side of the fretboard that is near you, so that your thumb is up in the air, and strum with the middle or index finger. The tip of your finger and fingernail brush the strings. This also can be done with the thumb when the hand is resting in the same position, but on the other side of the fretboard.

Two Fingers

Imitating a flat-picking sequence, try using the thumb to play the "one" strokes and the forefinger to play the "two" and "three" strokes. To do this, keep the palm of your hand resting on the fretboard just behind the bridge.

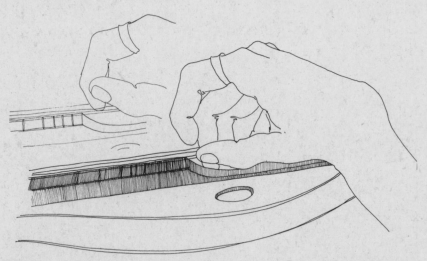

Three Fingers

This technique is essentially the same as the two-finger picking, except that the middle finger is used for the bass string and the index finger for the middle string. By using all three fingers, you smooth out the rhythm a great deal.

Experiment playing with all three fingers—with or without finger picks—making up different picking sequences, and adapting them to melodies. It might be a good idea to start with some of the simple songs with which you began strumming, and see how these songs lend themselves to finger-pickin'. You also might want to take a look at Earl Scrugg's bluegrass banjo instruction book for some further ideas on finger-pickin'.

Whole-hand or Claw Hammer

This is essentially a banjo style we have adapted to dulcimer playing. The hand doesn't move very much, and is more or less frozen into the position of the three-finger picking style. Brush your hand down across the strings with the fingernails of the four fingers. After the hand (as a unit) has passed the strings in a short arc, the thumb quickly flicks the strings on the upstroke as the entire hand moves up to its original position to begin another pass. The technique gives you a "trotting" sound—the thumb darts in and out producing a "bump-ditty-bump-ditty" effect.

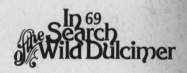

THE CLAW HAMMER

Semi-Flamenco

This style has similarities to both banjo and flamenco guitar techniques. The hand is held as for the Claw Hammer, except that the thumb does nothing but act as a launching pad from which the index finger springs. It's like knocking something off a table with a flick of your index finger—the thumb and index finger are held in the "OK" position, and the rest of the fingers merely follow the index finger. You can alter this technique a little by flicking the thumb backward against the melody strings after each launching of the four fingers. The thumb kicks back and sounds the unisons after the first pass with the other fingers.

Since all of these are modified banjo styles, you might do well to ask an old-time banjo player to show you them in more detail.

Pinching (Plucking)

To pinch the strings, wedge your fingers between any of the strings with a short, straight downward stroke. Then, on pulling up and away, you pinch the strings with the thumb and index finger to voice them. This plucking technique produces a very delicate quiet sound...something like a harpsichord. It works well for slower music in which the instrument occasionally accompanies the voice.

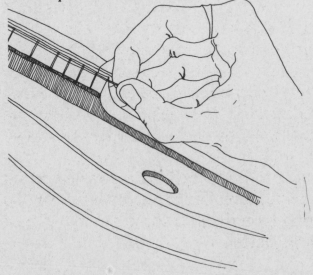

A-Bit-Like-Spanish-or-Classical-Style-Guitar

Brace your thumb against the side of the fretboard, and with your middle and index fingers pick back on the strings toward the thumb. Try to keep your fingers extended and move them as if they were two little legs plucking the strings. Try to play the strings individually as much as possible, without sounding them all together.

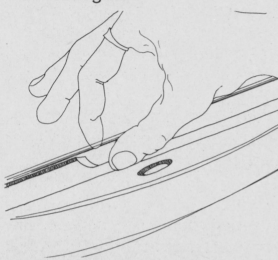

BEATING, SCRAPING, BANGING, AND OTHER SPECIALTY STYLES

Beat, scrape, or bang on the strings with whatever catches your imagination. You can use the noter, the flat of your hand, the side of a ripple-edged coin, a pencil, a violin bow...anything at all.

In the Appalachians some old-timers still play with a fiddle bow. If you use a bow, it is best to lay the instrument flat on your lap in Appalachian style and bow with the right hand, but we've heard of people holding the dulcimer vertically and using a bow, too— so do what you will.

You may be able to find a bow in a pawn shop or, of course, at a music store. Get some rosin, a resinous material fiddlers rub on their bows, to help your bow vibrate the strings better.

"Stop-Pickin'" is a specialty effect that you can produce with your right hand. A favorite with rock 'n' rollers, it is done by muting the strings with the palm of your right hand <u>immediately</u> after the stroke. Or, you can pick or strum with your upper wrist resting very lightly on the strings by the bridge. You'll find the effect of this stop-picking technique sounds like a Johnny Cash intro.

Slide, Bottleneck, and Steel-Guitar Styles

The slide, bottleneck and steel-guitar styles are three related ways of coming up with customized dulcimer sound. Since notes can be produced anywhere along the fretboard without depressing the strings to the frets, the sounds are quite unusual.

A bottleneck is a bottleneck. Cut it off near the top of the bottle, and be careful to leave enough room so that the glass will extend beyond the tip of whatever finger you use. Usually the middle or ring finger of the left hand is inserted into the bottleneck, from the top. For safety, we also suggest smoothing the sharp edge with a file and some emery paper.

Play notes by trailing the bottleneck behind the melody line itself. If the bottleneck is on your ring finger, your "lead fingers" (index and middle) can fret notes as usual, and the bottleneck provides a sliding chord sound when moved across the strings.

The slide method employs basically the same technique. The difference is that a metal bar—the slide—is held in the crook of the left hand between the ring and little fingers. Your lead fingers continue to fret notes as with the bottleneck method; however, you may find that you achieve more control with this independently held metal bar.

The same metal bar can be used for steel-guitar style playing. The difference is that in this method, the bar does all the fretting, and no lead fingers are used. Hold it any way that is comfortable in your left hand. You may find that your homemade bottleneck will work fine and you will not have to buy the metal slide. If you want to exert more pressure on the strings than the bottleneck allows, try using a small vanilla extract bottle partially filled with water, held lengthwise.

You will be able to make clean sounds anywhere on any string if you raise the strings off the fretboard about a sixteenth of an inch, and you can do this by replacing the nut with a slightly higher one. If you are going to use bottlenecking as an embellishment, you might not need to raise the strings very much, if at all. However, if you are going to use the steel-guitar technique a lot, raising the strings is necessary to produce a clear sound. You may even want to raise the bridge too, but this depends on your instrument. Strumming may sound odd if you're using the slide, so we'd recommend a flat-picking technique or finger picks.

The slide is great for blues, but the "minor third" tone (found halfway between the first and second frets in the Mixolydian mode) might not harmonize too well with the drones. Then again, it's all in how you listen.

Picks and Pickings From Other Cultures

One picking technique that interests us is used to play instruments like the Russian balalaika, the Arabian oud, and the bazooki, a Greek instrument. All these instruments require incredibly rapid playing, and their picking styles can be used to play the dulcimer. Use a triangular pick with slightly rounded corners. We prefer a thin pick which we choke-up on with our fingers, but maybe you'll find a thicker more inflexible pick works better. Hold it between the thumb and forefinger like this:

HOLDING THE PICK VERY TIGHTLY

Hold the pick tightly so that you can make short picking movements against the unisons. The motion you want to use is similar to that of using an eraser on the end of a pencil—back and forth very rapidly in short arcs at an angle to the strings. The pick's rounded corner helps you cross the strings evenly, so use it to your advantage. The sound you get will be very brisk, with brief notes.

Another pick we sometimes use is the mizrab, the pick used to play the Indian sitar.

THE MIZRAB

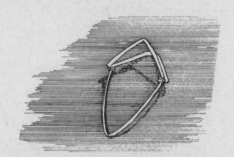

The mizrab is a thin wire finger pick which we usually place on the index finger. The wire part of the pick acts like a fingernail with which you pick and strum the strings. You may need to place your thumb against your index finger to keep the mizrab from falling off, if you do a lot of strumming with it. For picking, it allows a unique freedom of finger movement, and the sound takes on a shimmering quality.

If you use a mizrab, why not fashion a sitar-type bridge out of a piece of hardwood or bone? The trick is to allow the strings to "buzz" a little in the grooves. Maybe you only want to "buzz" the drones...so make the grooves larger than normal and see what you get.

Experiment.

Utilize what you can—strange materials, other parts of instruments from other cultures—and see where all this takes you.

It all boils down to folk music, and never forget, no matter what anyone says, that folk music is what you do.

8
Chording

Now we're getting into what all this has been building up to—chording.

Playing chords on the dulcimer opens your musical horizons and makes it possible for you to play a more harmonically complete melody line. Making chords usually involves depressing at least two of the strings at different frets and keeping one string open as a drone. Sometimes, however, all three strings are depressed on different frets—it depends on just what it is you want to do. Chording allows you to create a progression or series of related harmonic situations that serve to complement or enrich the melody, intensifying its natural expression and clarifying its direction.

You can play chords in most of the modes; however, once again, the Mixolydian is the most accessible. In this section our goal is not simply to spell out all the different chords, but rather to acquaint you with various fingerings you will need to effectively play melodic chords.

Usually the use of chords relates to the concept of harmony and, in turn, harmony relates to the modern twelve-tone chromatic scale. The use of chromatic notes really is not anything incredibly new, even though the consolidation and utilization of the full chromatic scale are relatively recent, having begun in the seventeenth century. In the fourth century B.C., the Greeks were using at least one "chromatic" note in their music. "Chroma," meaning color, is the word they applied to the series of tones consisting of A, F-sharp, F, and E. They called this series the Chromatic Tetrachord because of the F-sharp. Their other tetrachordal (four-note) scales did not have "colored" notes.

Once the monk Odo of Cluny systematized and labeled the modal scales in the tenth century, composers of religious music slowly began to juxtapose chant melodies and ranges of notes to achieve greater musical effects. Instead of having a choir sing the same note in unison, as in very basic Gregorian chanting, composers began separating the notes, eventually having voices sing two, three, and four tones simultaneously or in and around each other, creating <u>contrapuntal</u> as well as <u>polyphonic</u> (multi-toned) music.

Composers and musicians increasingly realized that some tonal relationships blended more readily, more harmoniously than others—some were "perfect concords," such as a root tone, a fourth, a fifth, and an octave; some were "imperfect concords" and only blended in specific instances, such as a third or sixth relationship; and some were out-and-out "discords," such as a second, a seventh, and sometimes a fourth.

By the end of the middle Renaissance in the 1400's, composers of both religious and secular music (including folk songs by troubadors) increasingly used chromatic notes to alter tonal relationships that did not work in the modal system; thus, the modes were altered for the sake of harmony.

To make tonal transitions smoother, the B of the Dorian and Lydian modes was often altered to a B-flat, making the Lydian a truly "major" scale and the Dorian a modern "minor" scale. Similarly, especially in secular music, the seventh tone of the Dorian and Mixolydian was sharpened to smooth the transition to the final resolving tone of the scale, the octave.

By the end of the sixteenth century all the modes had undergone chromatic alterations. Pure melody was not as interesting to composers as expanding polyphony and writing harmonic music. The five chromatic notes were accurately determined and developed during the Renaissance, and music was increasingly liberated from religious control. The Catholic Church attempted to revitalize the modes and the sanctity of music in the late Italian Renaissance by encouraging the work of Giovanni Palestrina and others. But it could not stop the rising tide of music by composers patronized by the nobility and wealthy merchants throughout Europe.

But, meanwhile, the people were also making music.

Think of a chord as a simultaneous voicing of several musical tones that create either concordant or dissonant harmony. The common chord is called a triad because it consists of three notes. Three elements make up every major triad—a tonic, or root tone, a major third, and a perfect fifth. A minor triad consists of a tonic, a minor third, and a perfect fifth—so the second element of any chord is very important to the overall sound of the chord. If the third tone is three whole intervals away from the root, the chord is major. But if the third is only two and a half intervals away, it is minor—just as in the scheme of the Aeolian mode in which the second interval is a half-step. When you lower a note a half-step you diminish the chord; if you raise a note a half-step, you augment it.

When the dulcimer is tuned to the Mixolydian mode, there are a limited number of possible complete triads with a root, a third, and a perfect fifth. You just can't play a full range of chords on the dulcimer—we only have an eight-tone scale. We can, however, play inversions (different note arrangements) of a few of these chords. Most often we rearrange two notes on either the unisons and middle string or middle and bass strings. So here's a new word for describing these two-note arrangements—diad.

This term isn't in music books because it really isn't legitimate, but it occurs to us that the majority of "chords" we play hardly ever consists of anything more than the bass drone (the octave of the tonic), and two notes a third or a fifth apart. (Sometimes we're daring and use a tonal relationship based on a fourth or sixth tone.) We call these chord inversions, these fragments, these elements of melodic harmonies, diads, because they really only have two tones when you get right down to it.

Keep in mind that you can use diads melodically to enhance a melody line, giving a song a fuller sound and a quality of strength and resolution.

To get into playing these chords, these diads, on the dulcimer, we'll start by numbering your fingers like this:

If you are to use the tips of your fingers to play a chord, we'll notate this with a capital "T," the number of the finger, and a circle around the notation. To show where this fingertip is placed, we'll locate the notation over the appropriate fret on the correct string.

The example means you place the tip of your middle finger on the unison strings at the fourth fret.

Now, if you are to lay one finger across all the strings to bar them, we'll show a "B," the number of the finger, and a circle around the notation, and place the notation over the fret to be barred.

In this case, lay your middle finger across the fretboard, depressing all the strings at the fourth fret. To add pressure to the bar, try placing a trailing left-hand finger (number 3) on top of the barring finger like this:

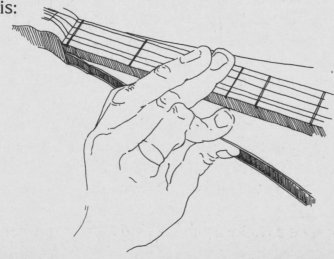

It's a good idea to have your fingernails cut short so that your contact with the strings is uniform. Also, take care to exert a steady fingertip pressure on the strings to produce the clearest sound. It's best to leave the index finger free for adding short slides, embellishments, and other notes while fingers two and three hold down the chord position itself. Some people use the thumb for making embellishments or reaching out for other notes, but we find this terribly awkward and don't recommend it.

For demonstration purposes we'll use the area around the third fret. As you move your chord configuration onto other frets, you'll find that they may become more major or minor, depending on the interval between the notes…but as you experiment with diads, you'll learn what sound is where on the fretboard. In the Mixolydian mode you won't run into any absolutely discordant tonalities, although some relationships will sound more pleasing than others. In the minor modes you will find discordancies—but, then again, remember it is our cultural musical conditioning that causes us to judge these tones as discordant. If someone complains, say you're working on avant-garde jazz dulcimer!

FINGERTIP CHORDS

This position is basic to playing diads on the unisons and middle string as well as the middle and bass. Most likely your ring finger is not very strong, so exercising this position may be a bit painful at first. Remember to press down firmly and accurately, because if you don't the chord will sound weak and watery. If your chords sound a bit sharp, it may be because your bridge is not accurately adjusted, so make sure your harmonic is over the octave fret. If you have a moveable bridge, take the time to adjust it carefully. If your bridge is fixed, you'll either have to live with everything being a trifle sharp, especially on the middle and bass strings, or perform the surgery recommended in Chapter One.

By moving your ring finger (3) from its position on the unisons to the same position on the bass, you get position I-B.

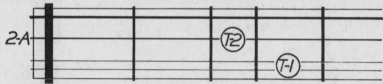

Keeping your middle finger (2) on the middle string at the third fret, place your index finger on the unison strings at the fourth fret, and get the reverse of I-A.

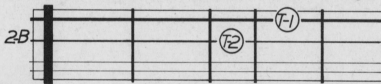

Again, by moving a finger to the bass string—in this case the index finger moves—you create the same diad using the bass and middle strings.

Now you can make a pleasant chordal transition by assuming the I-A position and then bringing your index finger into play to make a 2-A position.

This simple transition allows you to change chord structures without moving your entire hand—simply raise and lower your forefinger.

The I-A position can be played going up or down the scale, but make sure your fingers remain in the

same pattern. Try sliding I-A up the scale and listen to the tonal changes. Do the same with 2-A, and listen to the difference.

By maintaining the I-A position you can stretch out further than one fret with the index finger, as in illustration 2-D.

Again, by placing the index finger across the fretboard to the bass string you get a very major sounding triad—position 3-A.

And by pivoting on the middle finger (still at the third fret on the middle string), swivel your hand and reverse the positions of the index and third fingers. The ring finger moves to the bass string at the second fret, and the index finger moves to the unisons at the fourth fret, as in position 3-B.

These three sets of "fingertip" chords are basic to playing on more than one string. These diads can be played almost anywhere on the fretboard when tuned to the Mixolydian mode, and almost always your intervals will blend harmoniously. The half-fret intervals will show up as half-tones, so some positions will not blend with others. It's up to you, then, to work out progressions and melodies utilizing these fingerings. Experiment, and listen carefully to the sound combinations you make.

BAR CHORDS

When forming bar chords, the trailing fingers (usually the middle and fourth) of the left hand (fingers 2 and 3 in the illustration on p.79) come into play. These trailing fingers cover all the strings across a fret while the leading fingers play notes on other frets to complete the chord. So let's start by barring with the middle finger. Lay your middle finger across all the strings and exert an even pressure onto the first fret, making sure all the strings are depressed.

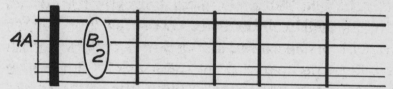

The sound you get should be very minor, like the Aeolian mode. You'll find it takes a good deal of pressure to keep all of the strings depressed to the frets so that the notes sound clean. You might even want to place your index finger on top of your middle finger to increase your downward pressure.

Now, starting on the first fret (the beginning of the Aeolian mode) bar all the frets up the scale and back.

The next fingering uses the ring finger (number 3 in our illustration) to bar, and the tip of the index finger in a position either one or two frets away from the bar. Here, the index finger stretches out to slide over these notes or to hold them. The trailing finger (3) bars the fret, sustaining the sound. The middle finger (2) is off the fretboard in this position. But if you do not want to slide the index finger back, as in position 4-B, the middle finger can come into play to depress the unisons onto the second fret.

When the index finger is two frets from the barred ring finger, the tip of the middle finger can bring the chord into a minor tonality if your fingers are placed like this.

Note that 4-C is another way to make a three-finger-tip chord. You can bring the chord into a major tonality if you move the entire structure so that the middle finger falls into the short-fret interval as in illustration 3-B.

Utilize bar chords along with fingertip chords and, once again, experiment with the patterns.

HUMDINGERS

These fingerings are rather hard to do and are little used—at least we haven't found much use for them—but they do come in handy when you are working with chords in other modes.

All these humdingers are self-explanatory, so let's start with 5-A and 5-B, which are reversals.

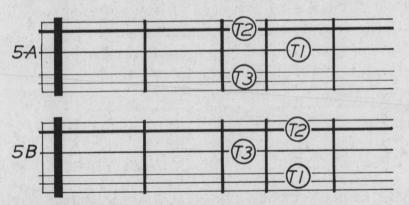

Position 5-C resolves to position 5-D, and this chordal resolve is found at other places up the fretboard too...so look for this around the octave note.

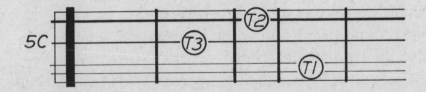

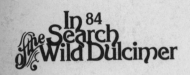

Position 5-E involves an unusually tricky finger change.

Position 5-F indicates how to play thirds, very pleasant intervals. You might easily deaden the middle string with your middle finger, so be careful when you depress the second of the unisons.

We rarely use the little finger, but you might find it helpful. Here's an example of how you can use it while the middle and ring fingers hold down a diad and the index and little finger trade notes. Try lifting one finger and then the other.

All these fingerings show how your fingers can work to your musical advantage if you exercise them by playing diads and chords. By no means have we covered all of the possible finger positions. However, we think we've given you enough material to work with so that you can go on from here.

If at some point you want to stop and analyze the notes of a particular chord or diad—do it. You'll be able to figure the notes out if you know for sure what

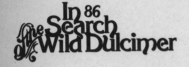

note your unisons are tuned to. If you have trouble, refer to the fretboard illustrations in Chapter Four. You might also want to purchase a book on music theory or work with a guitarist who can help you with working out chord progressions. In any event...it's up to you from here on in.

If you have a lute dulcimer, your chords will be very full and robust. Perhaps you may not want to keep tuning to an "open chord" like the Mixolydian mode, so why not place your strings at other values that enable you to form full-tone chords?

If you want to tune to a D-major triad, tune your unisons to D as usual, your middle to A as usual, and your bass string to an F-sharp. This tuning satisfies our definition of a triad, and all we've done is modified the tuning a little.

The same technique can be used with other starting tones, so see what happens when you get into it.

Invariably, your fingers will get sore and initially your hand will feel cramped from maintaining a steady pressure in unaccustomed finger positions. One way to exercise your fingers and hand is to learn the deaf-mute alphabet. Your hand will grow stronger from exercising the positions of this hand alphabet, which is explained in most dictionaries.

But there's nothing that beats practice for strengthening your hands and fingers. If you want to become proficient at playing chords on the dulcimer, you just have to keep on strumming—and the rewards will be commensurate with your devotions.

9
More
Odds and Ends:
The Locrian and Other Modes
Singing, Songsmithing, and Minstrelsy
An Apology and a Poem

Like history, we have ignored the Locrian mode because of its musical liabilities. But now that you have explored the six accepted modes, we'll show you the one history has thrown away. Once you understand this one, you are no longer a dulcimer musician, but a musician who plays dulcimer.

THE LOCRIAN MODE

The original keytone of the Locrian is B. The scale begins on the second fret, and has a scheme of ½—1—1—½—1—1. Its tuning looks like this:

$$***$$
$$\widehat{(X+2)}$$
$$X$$
$$X$$

The *** notation means that the bass string cannot be tuned within the established notation system of tuning from the unison value. Instead, tune the bass string an octave below the middle string when fretted on the fourth fret—but remember to tune the middle string to its $(X+2)$ value first.

Now, the odd thing about the Locrian mode is that it has no fifth tone. The bass provides a droning fifth only as an accompaniment. This doesn't help very much when you are looking for a resting place after playing a phrase, or trying to find a strong note from which to launch another phrase.

Since the dominant has been left out, the next strongest possible tone is the sub-dominant, the fourth. However, the relative minorness of the fourth combined with the octave fifth drones (carried by the other two strings) demands that you move off it quickly and seek a tone of completion. The only tones of completion, or resolve, are the octaves, so here is where you always wind up, which makes you feel as if you haven't gone anywhere at all. Maybe the Locrian should be called the "Sisyphus mode"—you may find yourself playing in circles.

Chording is a means of breaking out of the Locrian's circle. Yet when you chord a fifth from the middle string you break the mode and accomplish very little other than chording some sense into an otherwise very limited mode.

So try to work with the Locrian the way it is. Very quickly you'll employ all the techniques of melody, picking, rhythm and counterpoint—anything to break the monotony of the Locrian.

OTHER MODES

The seven "modern" modes (that is, the six accepted modes and the Locrian) came to life as we know them in the late sixteenth century. Before this, music was modal, but the modes were not exactly the same as today. So let's take a look at the Ecclesiastical modes, the ones that were reorganized and amended to produce our seven modern ones.

In the Ecclesiastical system there are four <u>authentic</u> modes (Dorian, Phrygian, Lydian, and Mixolydian), and four <u>plagal</u> modes identified by the term "hypo" meaning "under." All these modes were in use during the Middle Ages and into the Renaissance. Some were used more in theory than in practice, yet all of them consisted of a pentachord and a tetrachord, just like our modern ones.

An authentic mode consists of a pentachord with a tetrachord above it (e.g., the pentachord G,A,B,C, D and the tetrachord D,E,F,g.) A plagal mode consists of a tetrachord with a pentachord above it (e.g., beginning with a D'—that is, the D below the G below middle C—: D¦E¦F¦G,A,B,C,D), and most music theorists agree that plagal modes were devised to allow for melodies extending into the lower ranges. The main differences between authentic and plagal modes are that plagal modes begin a fourth lower than the authentic and that they have a different <u>dominant</u> (reciting tone); however, both modes share the same <u>final</u> note. The concept of the final became

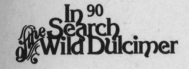

increasingly important in the development of music as the <u>form</u> of Gregorian chanting evolved from emphasizing the dominant (as in responsorial music) to emphasizing the final (as in antiphonal music, a development of melody in the eighth and ninth centuries).

In authentic modes the dominant is the hinge between the two segments of five notes and four notes; in the plagal modes, it is the perfect fourth that is the hinge—but the final is most important because it is the tone which resolves the melody.

To go further into the development and significance of plagal and authentic modes is beyond the scope of this book on dulcimer playing. Nonetheless, as best as we can determine, this is the way music shaped up at the beginning of the tenth century—when reading these charts (on p. 91), remember that capital letters refer to the G-scale that includes middle C and that lower case letters refer to the G-scale that is an octave above.

Because of the development of harmony and the use of chromatic notes, music was changed and secularized. The Catholic Church was losing control not only of the elements of music but also of the concepts behind music. In 1547 Glareanus, a music theorist, stated that there were fourteen possible and twelve usable modes. So of these six new modes, two were immediately rejected by musicians because they couldn't be used; two others seemed superfluous, so only two, the Aeolian and Ionian, were left—one very minor and one very major in tonality.

These new modes did not have designated dominants, because by this time music had progressed beyond having one note sung monotonously. Music was becoming fluid, melodic, harmonic, and varied in tone and structure. Most important, music was being composed for enjoyment and was already a part of the fabric of contemporary civilization. Soon after the disclosure of the six new modes, the Catholic Church decreed that music still was in the domain

Ecclesiastical Modes

				Range	Reciting Note	Final
1	First Mode	Auth.	Dorian	D-d	a	D
2		Plagal	Hypodorian	A-a	F	D
3	Second Mode	Auth.	Phrygian	E-e	b	E
4		Plagal	Hypophrygian	B-b	a	E
5	Third Mode	Auth.	Lydian	F-f	c	F
6		Plagal	Hypolydian	C-c	a	F
7	Fourth Mode	Auth.	Mixolydian	G-g	d	G
8		Plagal	Hypomixolydian	D-d	c	G

New Modes of the Sixteenth Century

		Range	Final
9	Aeolian	A-a	A
10	Hypoaeolian	E-e	A
11	Hyperaeolian ("over" aeolian, or Locrian)	B-b	B
12	Hyperphrygian	F-f	B
13	Ionian	C-c	C
14	Hypoionian	G-g	C

of the Church and the only modes allowed would be the Mixolydian, the Aeolian, the Ionian, the Dorian, the Phrygian, and the Lydian—but few people listened, and that's where it all ended.

So here we sit with dulcimers in hand. If you want simple music, uncomplicated music, here it is. If you want more complicated music, it began within these modes. If you want still more complicated music, you'd best go East.

SINGING

Open your mouth and let what is inside come out!

Initially this may seem difficult, but this difficulty will pass. Most people sing too low for their voice. They sing where it feels comfortable, which is usually

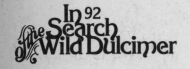

at a point of little exertion. Singing in a lower range doesn't develop your voice. Vocal chords must be explored, used, toned, pushed a little, and exercised like any other muscle in your body.

Sing where your voice stretches a little.

Take it easy, however. Don't overdo it at first. Ease into your voice. If you treat your voice well, it will shape up for you, but this doesn't happen overnight. Like learning to play the dulcimer, it takes time. You have to teach your voice, and the more you use it, the more you'll learn about its use.

Don't worry about pitch, and key, and carrying a tune. It's nice if you can carry a tune, but there's already been a Caruso and a Jenny Lind, and Ma Nature doesn't duplicate herself. So be what you are, and let that raucous sound roll out of your mouth.

If your voice always sounds like you are singing the dirty blues with a big rumbling sound—well, great! Sing the dirty rumbling blues.

Singing is a real joy, and anyone can do it. It's time to take the shower room into the streets. If, at first, you feel uncomfortable without your shower, then sing in the rain. But sing…outside, inside, on street corners, everywhere and anywhere.

Just sing.

SONGSMITHING

The prose-poem "Desiderata" says that "You are a child of the universe and have as much right to be here as anything else." If that's not a qualification for songsmithing, then we don't know what is.

Write what you feel, or think, or would like to feel or think; or think you'll feel if you like, or what you'll like if you feel you think…Put words to your melodies if you feel the need, and don't worry about making it all rhyme—work your words into the melody so it comes out, or work the melody into the words.

All you have to do is throw off a few paranoias.

MINSTRELSY

"More dulcimers came out of those hills than ever went into them..." And so it has been that the handful of people out of a thousand, and the hundred thousand out of a nation step away from the things they know, clinging only to a whispered promise in some half-remembered dream of themselves—something to be found in another valley or over another mountain. These are the minstrels.

Historically, they've permeated the fabric of mankind and woven it into a greater humanity. They took the thoughts, the events of one place and painted these stories for people of still somewhere else. Their tools were conversation, song, dance, music, and perhaps some laughter gathered at the expense of a joke on themselves. They have had many names and have worn many faces.

The twentieth century has brought us the perils and illusions of newer, faster communications, but now we have created new isolations, new xanadus, with different valleys, other mountains, and a new people with old eyes. Music, for some the liberator of the very personal spirit, has now become a race, a competition. The Musician has become an institutionalized, marketed commodity that is spoon-fed and fostered by a carefully watched electronic cult.

There is always a place to sleep, some food to eat, and sometimes even a little money for people whose lives bring peace.

AN APOLOGY AND A POEM

Here starts our apology: in as many cases as possible we have shifted the burden of teaching onto you, knowing that a book of this kind ultimately serves more as an information source and an encouragement than as a methodical teaching system. We've left out learning songs because we believe if you first learn

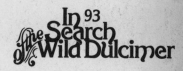

what the instrument is all about and then learn songs, you'll have a better grasp of the music within your-self, and it won't be so hard to get it out later on.

Admittedly, much of the history is colored to give you a feeling of what was happening in music many hundreds of years ago, and although we have not digressed from fact, we have written with a free license.

We have written, collected, researched, and rapped on people over several years and tens of thousands of hitch-hiking miles in all parts of the United States, and we realize we're a lot closer to the dulcimer and its music than when we began this journey.

The times we spent writing were often times we wanted to be playing. During one such period came these few lines that I hope will open for you our per-spective on this book.

My music lies sleeping.
When next it wakes, I'll be
A bird on Wing! And my
      Freedom
      Shall make everyone I
      Touch just a little more
         Free
         Themselves.
And when I land,
      When I touch down
      To clay feet
      And clay thoughts,
I pray some potter will come and remake me also.

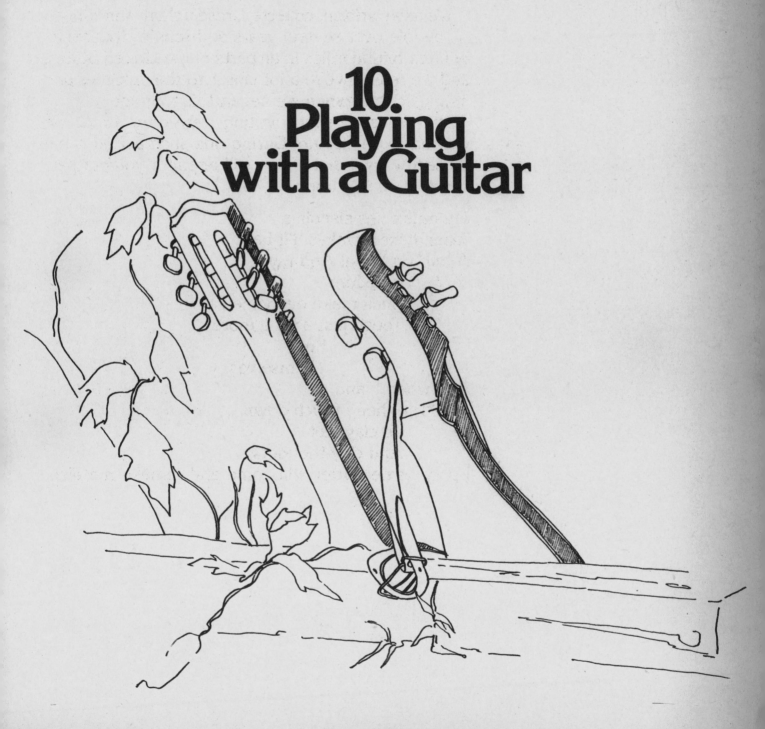

10.
Playing
with a Guitar

At some point you will probably want to play music with other musicians. This is not an uncommon desire, but for too long dulcimer players have been left out in the cold because nobody quite knew what to do with them. So, if you're planning on playing with a guitarist, here's some help for you and your friend from our friend Jake Bell.

Initially I thought this section should be called "What To Do When a Guitar Player Meets Up with a Dulcimer Player," and although this is not the title of this chapter, it still states the basic question.

Most guitarists don't immediately understand what modal music is all about, since they are not familiar with the jargon of dulcimer playing. Consequently, when faced with the problem of playing with a dulcimer, a guitarist might be at a loss to tell the dulcimer player what he should tune to. And you, the dulcimer player, might not have any idea what his instrument is all about either.

Now. Some alternatives.

The guitarist may put his guitar back into the case and quickly leave the scene, avoiding hours of mind-boggling explanations and counter-explanations leading to second thoughts about guitar playing that may cause him to consider taking up fly-fishing instead.

On the other hand, you both may make an attempt to work out your music and come to grips with the chromatic and modal musical approaches.

What you must always keep in mind is that your dulcimer is tuned modally, while the guitar is a chromatic instrument. It's got all the keys and all the notes. Your dulcimer has only the key in which you are tuned and the modal scale. Furthermore, as you know, you only have some of the notes he has, and you must determine which mode contains the notes of the tune of the song you both want to play.

The first thing you both should do is tune to the same keytone. If nothing else, at least the instruments will be tuned together. First tune the guitar.

It's very important that your friend's guitar be in tune, so let him get it right. Then, if the song you want to play is going to be in the Mixolydian mode, it's a good rule of thumb to tune the dulcimer to the key of D. So have your guitarist friend give you a D, and tune your unisons to this note. If he wants to play in E, fine. Your unisons will tune to an E just as well as D.

Now explain to your friend what the Mixolydian mode is. Simply put, it is the scheme of the G-major scale without the F-sharp; or, expressed another way, the scale of the Mixolydian mode has a minor seventh tone. Now he can go ahead and figure out the modal scale in D, or whatever, and he'll know what notes you have on your fretboard when you are tuned to the Mixolydian mode.

Here is a chart that might help him. When we worked it out, it helped me a great deal, so I'll pass it on. It's based on the Mixolydian mode transposed to the key of D.

Mode	Trad. Modal Key	Transposed Chromatic Key
Mixolydian	G	D
Aeolian	A-minor	E-minor
Locrian	B	F#-minor
Ionian	C	G
Dorian	D-minor	A-minor
Phrygian	E-minor	B-minor
Lydian	F	C

With this chart he can transpose the mode into the correct key. However, another problem may arise: often a song must be played in a particular mode because of the limitations of the string tensions and the fret arrangement of the dulcimer. To the guitarist the twelve keys and their scales and patterns are all available without changing the standard guitar tuning. But let's say you want to play a particular song in the Mixolydian mode keyed to D, and he only knows it in the key of C, with all its particular runs and chordal patterns. If he tries to play the song in

the key of D, all the patterns and runs which he has learned in C will be completely different. Once again, his alternatives are either to relearn the song in the key of D (using standard guitar tuning), improvise around the dulcimer as best he can, "bar" the changes or, better yet, use a capo.

In our example, he might want to place the capo on the second fret of the guitar and play the runs and patterns as he had learned them in the key of C— which when capoed on the second fret is another position for the key of D. This happens because a chord changes in alphabetical order as it is barred up the neck of the guitar, just as notes change alphabetically as you proceed up the neck. Taking into consideration the half-step between the notes B and C and E and F, the C chord changes in the following manner:

First Position	Barred On										
	1st	2nd	3rd	4th	5th	6th	7th	8th	9th	10th	11th	12th
C		C#	D	D#	E	F	F#	G	G#	A	A#	B	C

In the meantime, you are kept happy because the song is still going to be played in the Mixolydian mode keyed to D.

Additionally, the chords C, F, and G comprise the "key of C." The F chord played while barred on the third fret is another position of G; the G chord played while barred on the second fret is another position of A; and the C chord played while barred on the second fret is another position of D. The chords D, A, and G, then, comprise the "key of D." The same musical logic works for other modes and other keys. If you've gotten this far and can do it, the other modes and their chromatic relationships will fall readily into place.

By all means, experiment. Dulcimers and guitars can be played together as long as each musician understands where the other instrument is coming from.

Good luck.

11
Some Useful Charts, Books, and Records of Interest

This section is designed for quick reference. It's a consolidation of the essential information explained in previous sections on tuning, along with graphic information useful for dealing with strings, tuning ranges, modal schemes, and chromatic relationships. Because this book could never cover everything on dulcimers, we also include a list of some of the books and records you may want to get into for songs and folklore about the instrument.

THE MODAL NOTATION SYSTEM

To facilitate tuning into the various modes, always consider the first and second strings, the unison or melody strings, as the value "X" when played open; that is, without any being depressed to a fret. Counting up the scale from the open X note-value, each fret assumes a value of $X+1$, $X+2$, $X+3$, $X+4$, etc., according to its position on the fretboard.

DIATONIC FRETBOARD WITH TUNING NOTATION VALUES

| $X+1$ | $X+2$ | $X+3$ | $X+4$ | $X+5$ | $X+6$ | Octave | .... |

Tune the unisons to a workable pitch—some note that sounds good to you and is not watery or weak sounding. On the other hand, you shouldn't tune them inordinately tight. The middle and bass strings (third and fourth) are then tuned off the unisons by fretting the unisons at the appropriate numbered intervals along the fretboard. The only tone you have to recognize is the <u>octave</u> relationship (eight tones below the starting tone). All relationships are figured from the melody strings through octave values. (Only in tuning the Lydian and the Locrian will you have to tune the bass string off the middle string, a non-unison value.)

Example: (Read from bottom to top)

Ⓧ
Ⓧ+4
X
X

In Search of the Wild Dulcimer 100

Start by tuning the "X" strings until taut and up to the desired pitch. Then count four frets up the scale to the X+4 position, and fret the unisons there. Now tune the middle string (the third string on a four-string dulcimer) to that note but an <u>octave lower</u> than what you hear. To indicate that its value is an octave below X fretted on the fourth fret, it's circled. In this example, the fourth string (the bass string) is to be tuned to an octave below the unison strings when they are tuned to X; therefore, simply tune the bass string to the same note you tuned the unisons to, but make the bass note an octave lower. To show its relationship to the unisons, it's circled to indicate octave.

If you find it terribly difficult to hear the octave-fifth tone you need for tuning the middle string, you might try tuning the bass string after you've tuned your unisons, and then fret the bass string on the fourth fret. This will give you the correct note for the middle string, although its sound-color will be somewhat different.

In brief, the rules to follow are:

1 Tune the unisons first to any sound you like, and call that note you've tuned to "X."
2 Always tune to octave values.
3 Always tune the other strings to the unisons at the octave values indicated by X+1, X+2, X+3, etc., as designated in the Range and Tuning Guide. And in the case of the Lydian and Locrian modes, note the exceptions to the general rule.

STRING TONE TOLERANCES AND RANGE AND TUNING GUIDE

Together, these two charts will enable you to customize the sound of your dulcimer. If your instrument is shorter or longer than the twenty-four-inch string length used to compute these tonal ranges, you'll

String Tone Tolerances

Unwound

Gauge	Low	High
.010	F#	A#
.012	F	G#
.013	D#	G
.015	C#	F#
.016	C#	F
.017	**C** *	F
.018	B	D#
.020	A	C#
.021	G#	C
.022	G	B
.024	E	G#
.026	D	G

Wound

Gauge	Low	High
.018	A	D
.022	E	A
.024	D#	G#
.026	D#	G
.030	C	F#
.032	C	F
.034	B	D#
.036	A	D
.038	G	C
.042	G#	B
.044	G	B
.046	F#	A#
.048	F	A
.052	D#	G#
.055	C#	F#
.057	C	F

* Middle C

have to experiment, keeping in mind that for lengths over twenty-four-inches, a lighter gauge than the one listed will be needed to bring you up to the desired pitch. The pitches listed after a given gauge tell you between what frequencies the strings will resonate with the maximum tone.

Range and Tuning Guide:

Mode	Tuning	Scheme	First Note of Scale	Original Tonality	Note Tolerance low to high (Middle **C** set in bold face)				
Myxolydian	(X) (X+4) X X	11½11½1	Open Fret	G	Bb F Bb Bb	B F# B B	C G **C** **C**	D A D D	E B E E
Ionian	(X) (X+3) X X	11½111½	3rd Fret	**C**			C F C **C**	D G D D	E A E E
Aeolian	(X+1) (X+5) X X	1½11½11	1st Fret	A	C G Bb Bb	C# G# B B	D A **C** **C**	E B D D	
Dorian	(X+1) (X+4) X X	1½111½1	4th Fret	D	C F Bb Bb	C# F# B B	D G **C** **C**	E A D D	
Phrygian	(X+2) (X+5) X X	½111½11	5th Fret	E	D G Bb Bb	D# G# B B	E A **C** **C**	F# B D D	
Lydian	(X+6)* (X+3) X X	111½11½	6th Fret	F			Bb F **C** **C**	C G D D	D A E E
Locrian	** (X+2) X X	½11½111	2nd Fret	B				C# F# D D	D# G# E E

*The X+6 is a double octave value below X

**This note cannot be tuned from the melody strings (X) Tune it to an oclave below the 3rd string fretted on the 4th fret

Given a 24" string length and the premise that for gauges 10, 12 and 22, the maximum tonal range lies within those stated for the Myxolydian.

ENHARMONIC TRANSPOSITIONS

Given any starting keytone, this chart tells you what chromatic notes you have in any modal scale. Read across, left to right, this chart transposes the designated mode written on the fretboard at the top into any keytone.

For instance, run your finger down from the space marked Dorian. Each one of the boxes you cross could be a different starting tone than the original keytone of the Dorian mode, which is D, as indicated on the Modal Base Scale section running across the chart.

Enharmonic Transpositionings ~

Myxolydian (open)		Aeolian	Locrian	Ionian	Dorian	Phrygian	Lydian	Myxolydian
C		D	E	F	G	A	A#/B♭	C
C#/D♭		D#/E♭	F	F#/G♭	G#/A♭	A#/B♭	B	C#/D♭
D		E	F#/G♭	G	A	B	C	D
D#/E♭		F	G	G#/A♭	A#/B♭	C	C#/D♭	D#/E♭
E		F#/G♭	G#/A♭	A	B	C#/D♭	D	E
F		G	A	A#/B♭	C	D	D#/E♭	F
F#/G♭		G#/A♭	A#/B♭	B	C#/D♭	D#/E♭	E	F#/G♭
G		A	B	C	D	E	F	G
G#/A♭		A#/B♭	C	C#/D♭	D#/E♭	F	F#/G♭	G#/A♭
A		B	C#/D♭	D	E	F#/G♭	G	A
A#/B♭		C	D	D#/E♭	F	G	G#/A♭	A#/B♭
B		C#/D♭	D#/E♭	E	F#/G♭	G#/A♭	A	B

Modal Base Scale

If you want to know what notes the Dorian mode will have if you used B as the keytone, run your finger down five boxes under the column marked Dorian until you come to the box labeled "B." Then reading left to right continuously, your notes will be "B, C#, D, E, F#, G#, A, B." (Note that when you come to the end of the line on the right, you continue on the far left of that line.)

Where there are two notes in the same box separated by a slash mark (/), the top note is the sharp and the bottom is the flat. Sharps and flats are never read together in the same scale. An F-sharp is generally considered the same as a G-flat, although this is not strictly true; however, there are few musicians who can actually tell otherwise. (For the sake of "even-tempered" scales, these sharp-flat tones have come to be synonymous in modern music systems and are known as enharmonic notes.)

Another thing this chart does is tell you the sharps or flats in each chromatic scale or key. Starting from any point and reading up and down, the appropriate sharps and flats are revealed. Remember that the major scale evolved to duplicate the tones of the Ionian mode, whose fixed scheme is $1-1-\frac{1}{2}-1-1-1-\frac{1}{2}$. Since the major scales are mirror images of the Ionian's scheme, count the Ionian's scheme to determine the elements of any major scale. Minor scales can be figured by following the fixed scheme $1-\frac{1}{2}-1-1-1-1-\frac{1}{2}$.

For example, say you want to know where the sharps are in the key of E. At any place on the chart find an E and read up or down, counting off the intervals $1-1-\frac{1}{2}-1-1-1-\frac{1}{2}$. Remember not to count the initial E as your first whole $(1-)$ tone. Following this procedure, you will see that the key of E consists of the notes $E-F\#-G\#-A-B-C\#-D\#-E$. In other words, the key of E has four sharps, and they appear on the second, third, sixth, and seventh tones of the scale.

BOOKS AND RECORDS OF INTEREST

There are a number of books published on playing (and building) the dulcimer. We're not going to cover all of them; instead, we're going to list three that we've found useful in some way, and leave it up to you from there.

Each of these books is a variation on the same theme—traditional dulcimer playing—and should be included in your personal library if you're into having books around.

The Dulcimer Book by Jean Ritchie

This is the most traditional and widely read book on dulcimer playing. Jean Ritchie and her family have been involved with dulcimers and Appalachian folk music for generations, and much of the material is really "family tradition." It's a good book for learning about the dulcimer's European history. It includes basic instructions and some songs.

Mountain Dulcimer by Howard Mitchell

This book is primarily concerned with explaining how to build your own dulcimer. The explanations are generally clear, without a lot of folk-pretension and ostentation, and the instructions for playing in a traditional style are readily understandable.

Four & Twenty by Lynn McSpadden

A very comprehensive book, as far as traditional dulcimer playing goes. It includes good instructions, songs that are musically interesting, and exploration into "progressive" picking styles, and a handy chord chart.

There is not a great deal of recorded dulcimer music. What there is, however, is usually of high-quality, and can be classified as traditional or contemporary.

Jean Ritchie's album, "Appalachian Dulcimer," (Folkways number 8352) is a fine collection of traditional Appalachian folksongs. Along similar lines is Howie Mitchell's album, Mountain Dulcimer, which serves to explain aspects of his book. You might want to purchase both the book and record as a set.

Possibly the finest traditional dulcimer playing that has ever been recorded is by Paul Clayton. He has a number of albums available, but Dulcimer Songs and Solos is truly outstanding. The music is diverse, the playing is artful and subtle, and his singing is beautiful. It is a Folkways album, number FG-3571.

Contemporary dulcimer music is best exemplified by the work of Mimi and Richard Fariña. These albums are really unique and the music is bright and lyrical. We'd recommend your buying these albums if you can. If you can't buy all of them, try to get the Best of Richard & Mimi Fariña—Vanguard #BSB 21/2. The others are: Memories—Vanguard #79263; Reflections in a Crystal Wind—Vanguard #79204; Celebrations for a Grey Day—Vanguard #79174; and Singer-Songwriter Project—Electra #EKS 7299.

ROBERT LEWIS FORCE, JR.

The way it all finally worked out, at one time or another I was the youngest in a family, the oldest in a family, an only child, a bachelor child, and a boarded child, and now I can lay claim to nineteen half- and stepbrothers and sisters. But at seventeen, I moved out on my own and began intensely spending $500 for wine that retailed for no more than $1.19 a fifth. Between then and twenty, I tried college, drugs, sex, and travel, in that order.

Eleven days before turning twenty, I won $18.50 in a poker game, decided it was time to learn how to play music, and went and bought a dulcimer from an Austrian immigrant violin maker who said he got the idea from a 1945 edition of Popular Mechanics.

In the next five years I got married and divorced, hitch-hiked 150,000 miles through forty-four states and seven foreign countries, taught myself to play the instrument, and set about communicating what I had learned to others.

My constant companions for the last three years have been a pack, sleeping bag, dulcimer, two changes of clothing and twenty-five pounds of notes and notebooks. My not-so-constant companion has been Al d'Ossché. We met at the 44th Annual North Carolina Fiddlers' Convention through the mutual discovery that out of the 50,000 people in attendance, we were the only dulcimer players. Together, we've played on television and radio, at folk and bluegrass festivals, coffeehouses, colleges, street corners and subway stations.

During these times, people have asked us to show them how to do what we do. So we hauled out the twenty-five pounds of notes, analyzed them, boiled them down, analyzed ourselves, got boiled ourselves, wrote, rewrote, changèd, added to, wrote, and rewrote this book.

ALBERT KEMPTON, CONRAD D'OSSCHÉ

Once it was all simple and straightforward. But at eleven, I was living in California and was sent to study in New England; at eighteen it was college in North Carolina, and at twenty-two it was to be law school. But somewhere along the way certain things began to make increasingly more sense as others made less, and as nature abhors a vacuum, dulcimer playing began to occupy more of my time.

I left North Carolina diplomaed but dulcimerless. My first instrument (a three-string "flat-land tourist special") found its way into my life while I was living in self-induced exile six miles from the Canadian frontier in northern Vermont. After a few months of solitude, and the prospect of an intense Vermont winter, I decided to take a hint from the migrating geese and head south where I belonged. This notion was dramatically confirmed one morning when I woke to find my dulcimer's strings resplendent with tiny icicles and my old convertible covered with more than a foot of snow.

It was to Washington, D.C., that I went, and at just about this time, Bob and I careened into each other's lives and found that our techniques and music were somehow forming along similar lines.

I began adding to the ever-enlarging pack of notes and was seen lugging parts of them around in a backpack. Later we went to Munich, where we wrote the original manuscript, built dulcimers in a friend's kitchen, and lived the emigré life.

While Bob continued his travels, I lived in northwest Connecticut building dulcimers, teaching dulcimer at a local school, and reworking In Search of the Wild Dulcimer. But now that this book is in your hands, I've hit the road again, too...and so it goes.